Domestic Violence

Tamara L. Roleff, *Book Editor*

David L. Bender, *Publisher*
Bruno Leone, *Executive Editor*
Bonnie Szumski, *Editorial Director*
David M. Haugen, *Managing Editor*

OPPOSING
VIEWPOINTS®
SERIES

Greenhaven Press, Inc., San Diego, California

Cover photo: Irene Zevgolis

Library of Congress Cataloging-in-Publication Data

Domestic violence : opposing viewpoints / Tamara L. Roleff, book editor.
    p.   cm. — (Opposing viewpoints series)
    Includes bibliographical references and index.
    ISBN 0-7377-0346-6 (lib. bdg. : alk. paper). —
ISBN 0-7377-0345-8 (pbk. : alk. paper)
    1. Family violence. I. Roleff, Tamara L., 1959– . II. Opposing
viewpoints series (Unnumbered)
HV6626.D668 2000
362.82'92—dc21   99-047825
                                              CIP

Greenhaven Press, Inc., P.O. Box 289009
San Diego, CA 92198-9009

"Congress shall make no law. . . abridging the freedom of speech, or of the press."

First Amendment to the U.S. Constitution

The basic foundation of our democracy is the First Amendment guarantee of freedom of expression. The Opposing Viewpoints Series is dedicated to the concept of this basic freedom and the idea that it is more important to practice it than to enshrine it.

Contents

Why Consider Opposing Viewpoints?

"The only way in which a human being can make some approach to knowing the whole of a subject is by hearing what can be said about it by persons of every variety of opinion and studying all modes in which it can be looked at by every character of mind. No wise man ever acquired his wisdom in any mode but this."

John Stuart Mill

In our media-intensive culture it is not difficult to find differing opinions. Thousands of newspapers and magazines and dozens of radio and television talk shows resound with differing points of view. The difficulty lies in deciding which opinion to agree with and which "experts" seem the most credible. The more inundated we become with differing opinions and claims, the more essential it is to hone critical reading and thinking skills to evaluate these ideas. Opposing Viewpoints books address this problem directly by presenting stimulating debates that can be used to enhance and teach these skills. The varied opinions contained in each book examine many different aspects of a single issue. While examining these conveniently edited opposing views, readers can develop critical thinking skills such as the ability to compare and contrast authors' credibility, facts, argumentation styles, use of persuasive techniques, and other stylistic tools. In short, the Opposing Viewpoints Series is an ideal way to attain the higher-level thinking and reading skills so essential in a culture of diverse and contradictory opinions.

In addition to providing a tool for critical thinking, Opposing Viewpoints books challenge readers to question their own strongly held opinions and assumptions. Most people form their opinions on the basis of upbringing, peer pressure, and personal, cultural, or professional bias. By reading carefully balanced opposing views, readers must directly confront new ideas as well as the opinions of those with whom they disagree. This is not to simplistically argue that everyone who reads opposing views will—or should—change his or her opinion. Instead, the series enhances readers' understanding of their own views by encouraging confrontation with opposing ideas. Careful examination of others' views can lead to the readers' understanding of the logical inconsistencies in their own opinions, perspective on why they hold an opinion, and the consideration of the possibility that their opinion requires further evaluation.

Evaluating Other Opinions

To ensure that this type of examination occurs, Opposing Viewpoints books present all types of opinions. Prominent spokespeople on different sides of each issue as well as well-known professionals from many disciplines challenge the reader. An additional goal of the series is to provide a forum for other, less known, or even unpopular viewpoints. The opinion of an ordinary person who has had to make the decision to cut off life support from a terminally ill relative, for example, may be just as valuable and provide just as much insight as a medical ethicist's professional opinion. The editors have two additional purposes in including these less known views. One, the editors encourage readers to respect others' opinions—even when not enhanced by professional credibility. It is only by reading or listening to and objectively evaluating others' ideas that one can determine whether they are worthy of consideration. Two, the inclusion of such viewpoints encourages the important critical thinking skill of objectively evaluating an author's credentials and bias. This evaluation will illuminate an author's reasons for taking a particular stance on an issue and will aid in readers' evaluation of the author's ideas.

As series editors of the Opposing Viewpoints Series, it is our hope that these books will give readers a deeper understanding of the issues debated and an appreciation of the complexity of even seemingly simple issues when good and honest people disagree. This awareness is particularly important in a democratic society such as ours in which people enter into public debate to determine the common good.

Those with whom one disagrees should not be regarded as enemies but rather as people whose views deserve careful examination and may shed light on one's own.

Thomas Jefferson once said that "difference of opinion leads to inquiry, and inquiry to truth." Jefferson, a broadly educated man, argued that "if a nation expects to be ignorant and free . . . it expects what never was and never will be." As individuals and as a nation, it is imperative that we consider the opinions of others and examine them with skill and discernment. The Opposing Viewpoints Series is intended to help readers achieve this goal.

David L. Bender & Bruno Leone,
Series Editors

Greenhaven Press anthologies primarily consist of previously published material taken from a variety of sources, including periodicals, books, scholarly journals, newspapers, government documents, and position papers from private and public organizations. These original sources are often edited for length and to ensure their accessibility for a young adult audience. The anthology editors also change the original titles of these works in order to clearly present the main thesis of each viewpoint and to explicitly indicate the opinion presented in the viewpoint. These alterations are made in consideration of both the reading and comprehension levels of a young adult audience. Every effort is made to ensure that Greenhaven Press accurately reflects the original intent of the authors included in this anthology.

Introduction

"Children who witness violence between adults in their homes . . . have been called the 'silent,' 'forgotten,' and 'unintended' victims of adult-to-adult domestic violence."
—*Jeffrey L. Edleson*, Journal of Interpersonal Violence, *August 1999*

One of Indiana congressman Dan Burton's earliest memories is hearing his mother being beaten by his father. He was five or six years old, he writes, when he was awakened during the middle of the night by loud noises:

> I heard the sound of furniture being shoved across the room and a lamp crashing to the floor. Then I heard my mother's bloodcurdling scream. Every nerve in my body stood on end. Terrified, I lay there thinking, "My God, it's happening again." For almost a decade, my father beat my mother nearly every week. Anything seemed to set him off: jealousy, rage over something that hadn't gone his way. He'd start by saying horrible things to her. He'd rip her clothes off and throw her down. Sometimes he literally knocked her unconscious. Afterwards, her face and eyes would be swollen and bruised. He'd put wet cloths on her face to wake her up. I'd hear him consoling her, saying he was sorry, that it would never happen again. But of course it did.

Burton's story is a familiar one to the estimated 3 million to 10 million children who witness family violence in their homes every year. Although parents may try to hide the fights and beatings from their families, the children inevitably know what is happening. One child therapist compares children to a "highly sensitive recording device" that is "capable of remembering the abuse that occurs in his or her home" whether or not "he or she has witnessed it directly and whether or not abuse is openly discussed."

Many battered spouses rationalize their decision to stay with their abusers for "the good of the children." They believe that their children are better off emotionally and financially if the parents stay together, even if one of the parents is abusive. However, researchers have found that children exposed to domestic violence often suffer physical and psychological trauma as a result.

Children who witness family violence are themselves frequently victims of child abuse. Sociologists Murray A. Straus and Richard J. Gelles surveyed over 6,000 families and discovered that 50 percent of the men who battered their wives also abused their children. An earlier study by William Stacy and Anson Shupe found that child abuse was 15 times more likely to occur in families with a history of domestic violence.

Domestic violence advocates have long known that children of abusive parents often grow up to be abusive in their own relationships. According to Straus and Gelles, "the learning experience of seeing your mother and father strike one another is more significant that being hit yourself." They contend that boys who see their fathers beating their mothers learn that violence is an acceptable way to deal with anger and frustrations, that women are not worthy of respect, and that it is permissible to beat them. In *Behind Closed Doors*, Straus and Gelles state that boys who have witnessed domestic abuse between their parents are three times more likely to grow up and abuse their own wives than boys from nonviolent homes.

Likewise, the two researchers argue that experiencing and observing violence teaches girls that violence equals love—that being loved by someone also means being hit by them. They note that girls who grow up witnessing battering are also more likely to be abused as adults.

Being exposed to domestic violence may also cause behavioral and emotional problems in some children. Researchers who have studied the effects of domestic violence on children have found that it tends to make them aggressive and antisocial. Children who witness parental violence frequently act out against their younger or weaker siblings and classmates, and sometimes even against their mothers. A child's anxiety about parental violence may also be exhibited through general fearfulness, nightmares, confusion regarding parental loyalties, feelings of powerlessness, difficulty concentrating and poor school performance, substance abuse, running away from home, sexual promiscuity, and physical reactions such as stomach cramps, headaches, sleeping and eating disorders, and frequent illness.

Children in violent homes are also susceptible to feelings of low self-esteem, shame, guilt, and high levels of stress due to their beliefs that the violence is their fault, that they should be able to stop the beatings, and that they must keep the beatings a secret. Marya Grambs, who grew up watching her father beat up her mother, explains the confusion she felt over her parents' fights:

> At some point in the fights, [my father] would say, "if you say one more word, I'll hit you." And then my mother, by now pretty upset, would say something, and then he would throw her down, kick her, slap her, punch her, pull her hair.

> As a child always listening to the fights in the stairway leading to their bedroom, I would try out figure out who was right and who was wrong. I never could. He always seemed so right, so logical. Why did she say that one last thing? . . . I couldn't understand that the excessiveness of his reaction was what was wrong.

Therapists and researchers are quick to point out that not all children exhibit these problematic behaviors and emotions, and not all actions and feelings are exhibited in each child. Generally, the extent of a child's physical and psychological trauma is dependent on the child's age during the abuse and the length and severity of the abuse. Experts agree that the less violence a child sees and experiences, and the younger the child is, the less likely it is that he or she will develop problems later in life or continue the cycle of violence as an adult.

The problem of child witnesses to domestic violence—who may themselves continue the cycle of violence as adults—is an important issue in the debate over domestic violence. In *Domestic Violence: Opposing Viewpoints*, the authors examine the severity and prevalence of domestic violence and ways to prevent it in the following chapters: Is Domestic Violence a Serious Problem? What Factors Contribute to Domestic Violence? Are Legal Remedies Against Domestic Violence Just and Effective? How Can Society Help Victims of Domestic Violence? The viewpoints in this anthology offer insights into the motivations of batterers as well as solutions to end the violence.

CHAPTER 1

Is Domestic Violence a Serious Problem?

Chapter Preface

When police responded to a 911 call of "shots fired" at the home of *NewsRadio* actor and comedian Phil Hartman on May 28, 1998, they found both Hartman and his wife Brynn lying on their bed, dead of gunshot wounds. Police believe that Brynn had shot and killed her husband before they arrived, and then shot and killed herself as her children were removed from the house.

Those who knew the Hartmans were well aware that Brynn sometimes had trouble controlling her anger and flew into fits of rage. Some domestic violence experts contend that Phil Hartman's death is an extreme, but not unusual, example of female domestic violence against men. The U.S. Department of Justice reports that 38 percent of the victims of spousal homicide are men who were killed by their wives. Murray Straus, Richard J. Gelles, and Suzanne Steinmetz, sociologists and authors of *Behind Closed Doors: Violence in the American Family*, studied the incidence of domestic violence between men and women. They found that while 1.8 million women were the victims of domestic violence each year, two million men were assaulted by their intimate partners. Since then, nearly thirty studies have supported the conclusions of Straus, Gelles, and Steinmetz that women are as violent as men.

Although women's advocates concede that men are also victims of domestic abuse, they maintain that female violence against men is usually either in self-defense or in retaliation for male abuse against them. Moreover, they assert, a man punched by a woman is unlikely to suffer as much pain or chance of injury as a woman who is punched by a man. Even when the male partner is injured, researchers found that women suffered injuries that were nearly three times as severe as the men's injuries. Therefore, many sociologists and women's advocates reject the claim that women are as violent as men.

The question of whether male battering by women is as serious a problem as female battering by men is just one of the issues examined in the following chapter, as authors debate the nature, extent, and severity of domestic violence.

"A person is battered every 15 seconds in America by a spouse or a cohabitator."

Domestic Violence Is a Serious Problem

Marva Bledsoe

Marva Bledsoe argues in the following viewpoint that family violence is a serious problem that negatively affects many Americans of all races, ages, and income levels. Furthermore, she asserts, domestic violence is a learned behavior; many children who witness abuse falsely believe that violence is normal and is to be expected in their own adult relationships. The secrecy surrounding family violence must be exposed before society can find a solution to reducing domestic abuse. Bledsoe is the executive director of the Women's Resource Center in Oceanside, California.

As you read, consider the following questions:
1. According to Bledsoe, how frequently is a person battered in the United States?
2. What percentage of spouse-abusing families abuse their children as well, as cited by the author?
3. What is one reason that family violence continues to thrive in the United States, according to Bledsoe?

Reprinted, with permission, from "Domestic Violence Grows as Other Crime Drops," by Marva Bledsoe, *San Diego North County Times*, October 5, 1997.

Violent crime is a major problem in this country. The possibility that any of us might be injured or have our homes invaded by a stranger is frightening to contemplate.

But hundreds of thousands of Americans face an even more devastating reality. They are harmed, not by strangers, but by those they trust and love. They are victimized, not on the street or in the workplace, but in their own homes.

The place where they should feel safe and secure has become instead a place of danger. The shadow of family violence has fallen across their lives and they are forever changed. . . .

A Serious Problem

The following data from the California attorney general, United States Department of Justice and Women's Resource Center help to illustrate the seriousness of family violence in our nation:

- A person is battered every 15 seconds in America by a spouse or cohabitator.
- One in four murders nationwide involves family relationships.
- In California, one in two female homicide victims is murdered by her spouse.
- Half of the nation's couples have already had at least one violent incident.
- Sixty-three percent of boys ages 11–20 who commit homicide kill the man who is beating their mother.
- One out of four high school dating relationships is violent.
- Violence is a common occurrence in 10–25 percent of all marriages in the United States.
- In half of spouse-abusing families, the children are battered as well.
- Abuse-related absenteeism results in an estimated economic loss to the country of $3 billion to $5 billion per year, plus another $100 million in medical expenses.
- Five percent of the victims of spousal violence are male.
- Twenty-five percent of all women who are beaten are pregnant.
- Seventy percent of all assault cases involve spousal abuse.

• One-third of all hospital emergency room visits are domestic violence-related.

The Family and Society Are Threatened

Domestic violence cuts across all racial, age and economic lines and shatters families at every level of our social structure. Violence within the family affects the lives of all family members, threatens the entire community and causes a special kind of agony.

The trauma goes beyond the pain of any one episode. Once begun in a relationship, a pattern of violence will escalate both in frequency and severity. Worse, abuse in the home today leaves its mark on the future. Family violence is cyclical in nature, and to continue to tolerate abuse in the family is to assure a violent future.

Rob Rogers. Reprinted by permission of United Feature Syndicate, Inc.

Domestic violence has no single cause or simple solution. And while it is now being recognized and acknowledged as an important social problem, there is much to be done. Family violence continues to thrive in part because society is unaware of the nature and extent of the problem. A lack of understanding of the nature of family violence encourages those involved to carefully keep a cloak of secrecy in place.

Public awareness of the issues of family violence offers hope that we can bring the problem out into the open and affect the incidence of such violence. Spousal assault is everyone's concern. We must find solutions to this problem together.

There Is Hope

If you know or suspect that someone is being abused, tell that victim that there are alternatives, there are choices, there is hope.

If you know or suspect that someone is an abuser, tell that person that without help, the problem will only get worse.

> *"The [domestic violence] figures sound horrific, but they derive from the same factory of outrageous statistics which produced the notorious claim that 30 . . . percent of American women are victims of incest."*

The Seriousness of Domestic Violence Is Exaggerated

Philip Jenkins

In the following viewpoint, Philip Jenkins argues that the rise in the number of reports of domestic violence is due to women's increased awareness of the availability of social services and their willingness to use the services, not because of an actual increase in the behavior itself. In addition, Jenkins contends that the extent of domestic violence is determined by how "abuse" is defined. Broadening the definition increases the number of cases, he asserts. Jenkins is a professor of history and religious studies at Pennsylvania State University, and the author of numerous articles on crime and religion.

As you read, consider the following questions:
1. What have battered women's advocates misleadingly called the "day of dread for women," according to Jenkins?
2. In the author's opinion, how should "abuse" be defined?
3. How has the definition of domestic "abuse" been expanded, according to the author?

Excerpted from "Abusing the Spousal Abuse Laws," by Philip Jenkins, *Family in America*, June 1997. Reprinted by permission of the Rockford Institute.

L ike child sexual abuse, battering is seen as a basic means of intimidation by which patriarchal society maintains its power, and both—according to feminists—are near-universal female experiences: the family is an instrument of physical and psychic repression. In her pioneering 1976 text on the matter, Del Martin wrote that "The economic and social structure of our present society depends upon the degradation, subjugation and exploitation of women"; or to quote the elegant sentiment of Karen De Crow, former head of the National Organization for Women, "men have emerged from caves, and are now using physical force in the suburbs." Women need "refuges" or "shelters" not merely from one specific abuser, but from the violence of the whole male society. Since the family institution is so corrupt, so repressive, no worthwhile change can be expected from within. The powerless can only be protected by means of external intervention, by the state and its social-service agencies. . . .

Expanding Social Services

Though feminists brought the battering issue into the political mainstream, they were consciously or otherwise working in close alliance with another trend of the 1980s and 1990s, namely the vast growth of social-service agencies in the aftermath of the 1960's "Great Society." Social-welfare expenditures by federal and state authorities rose from less than 12 percent of gross national product (GNP) in 1965 to over 20 percent a decade later, and the number of clinical social workers exploded, from 25,000 in 1975 to 80,000 by 1990. Expanding agencies gained strength from ever more intrusive powers to seek out social dysfunctions, especially the laws requiring doctors, teachers, and other professionals to report suspected child abuse or family violence. Though activists knew better, they claimed to believe that rising reports of abuse and violence actually reflected a real growth in the behavior itself, which justified further intervention, which in turn generated still more reports. The spiral became self-sustaining, and potentially infinite.

The issue on which other campaigns were modeled was that of baby-battering or child *physical* abuse, which from the late 1960s was portrayed as an enormous problem that could threaten any child in any type of home; the statistics, however troubling, represented only the tip of the iceberg, while solutions to the problem were thwarted by a general refusal to acknowledge that such appalling acts could occur. A hidden epidemic could be cured only by creating specialized groups or agencies with both the will and the power to intervene. From about 1976, these same ideas were increasingly applied to the phenomenon of spouse abuse, which was similarly portrayed as an "epidemic," a growing "crisis," on the strength of changes in reporting. In Massachusetts, for example, the number of calls to abuse hotlines rose from 35,000 in 1985 to 88,000 in 1992. This increase was seriously discussed in the papers as an index of the terrifying rise of battering, urgent proof that "rising violence against women must stop," to use a typical headline. Of course it is no such thing, as the rise rather reflects improved awareness of available services, and a greater willingness to describe as abuse conduct that would formerly have escaped official attention. This was well-demonstrated in 1994 when the publicity accorded the O.J. Simpson case led to an unprecedented upsurge of calls to spouse-abuse hotlines, without any suggestion that actual behavior had changed in any way.

But the process of increased reporting continues as agencies proactively seek out signs of possible abuse. Since 1992, the American Medical Association has decreed that all doctors should screen women patients for what they believe to be signs of domestic violence or abuse, for example by asking women if a partner has ever made them feel afraid. Doctors are advised to introduce this topic with a simple "noncontroversial" phrase, which is in fact politically loaded to an incredible degree: "Because abuse and violence are so common in women's lives, I've begun to ask about it routinely." Several states place counselors, generally drawn from local women's shelters, in emergency rooms to observe possible signs of domestic violence. As such individuals are usually drawn from the ranks of the most inflexible and ideological feminist activists, the likelihood of over-diagnosis is enormous, but the resulting statistics will be fed into the insatiable maw of media anxious to hear about the deepening crisis. From the mid-1980s, it was a truism that domestic abuse constituted an "epidemic," demanding the broad public-health responses which would be required for any other plague. Since the 1980s, the U.S. Congress has repeatedly held hearings on this "public health" aspect, providing platforms for some of the starkest attacks on the evils of the nuclear two-parent family.

Loose Use of "Abuse"

Though the frequency of domestic violence has almost certainly been declining for decades, the figures are used to present the contrary "epidemic" view, and they are usually encapsulated in memorable factoids: "every 18 seconds a woman is beaten by her partner," or, "almost four million American women were physically abused by their husbands or boyfriends in the last year alone." The figures sound horrific, but they derive from the same factory of outrageous statistics which produced the notorious claim that 30 (or 40, or 50) percent of American women are victims of incest—but that is another story. Sometimes the evidence used for such claims is so transparently ludicrous that even journalists—those most naively trusting of beings—can recognize its bogus quality. In 1993, women's refuges and pressure groups throughout the United States declared that they were on alert for the Super Bowl game, as frustrated men were then most likely to take out their anger on their partners, and special advertising was launched to urge the brutes

---

Domestic Violence Factoid

Sixty-three percent of young men between the ages of 11 and 20 who are serving time for homicide have killed their mother's abuser.

This factoid is often used by [battered women's advocate] Sarah Buel in her speeches. It appears to be yet another fact from nowhere. The FBI has published no data that supports this claim. The FBI's Uniform Crime Reports has no tables that report on prison populations, let alone a table or figure that breaks down prison populations by age of offender and relationship to victim. There are no Department of Justice reports that report on what number or percentage of young men kill their mother's batterer.

Richard J. Gelles, "Domestic Violence Factoids," 1995.

---

to control themselves on this "day of dread for women." It rapidly emerged that the claim was wholly spurious, and that no evidence whatsoever linked the Super Bowl to any rise (or fall) in battering. But the claim had its brief spell of fame, and no doubt the idea will reappear in the literature for decades to come, as what gardeners call a hardy perennial.

The inflation of claims is achieved by an ever-expanding definition of abuse. The word "abuse" means little in itself beyond the perception that something is not being used or treated appropriately, but years of association have contextualized it alongside acts of violence and sexual exploitation, especially those committed against the defenseless. We all know that domestic abuse means (or should mean) acts of physical violence, the crimes of beating, battering, kicking, even the outright torture recorded in the most horrific instances; but this is absolutely not the limit of the "abusive" behaviors listed by advocates, which are employed to produce the memorable statistics in which people describe their experience of victimization. An effective sleight-of-hand came into play here, as "abuse" was substituted for the words "beating" and "battering," ostensibly to comprehend the broad range of types of exploitation. The problem is that abuse is so generic a term that it lends itself to almost any hostile act, but is reported as if it involved the most blood-curdling attack with a knife or a poker. Linked to this is the notion of inevitable escalation, that every form of "abuse" is a first step which will all but inevitably lead to mayhem or murder. From this perspective, there is no such thing as "minor" abuse, and even to use the phrase suggests a frightening callousness towards female suffering. How dare anyone question the self-evident sequence that leads from words to bullets?

Trivializing Abuse

One much-used graphic that appears in countless books and pamphlets derives from an "Intervention Project" based in Duluth, Minnesota, and explains the varieties of abuse: certainly, physical acts are represented, but so is "using male privilege," defined as "making all the big decisions. Acting like the master of the castle." "Intimidation" includes "using looks . . . gestures, loud voice" to dominate a woman. This list is shocking in its trivialization of the concept of abuse, and its cynical attempt to misuse justified public anger against violence to attack these other, far more subjective acts. The idea of abuse is shamelessly being abused here, as in so many other documents in which raising one's voice in anger is listed as a form of domestic abuse. The problem is sufficiently serious without cynical inflation of this kind. A golden rule in interpreting statistics is always to demand from the very start a definition of terms. If it is claimed that *x* percent of women are abused or harassed, or *y* percent of men come from dysfunctional families, we should always ask what terms like "abuse" and "harassment" and "dysfunctional" actually signify. The answer is usually that they mean whatever the speaker wishes them to mean. We could all benefit from reading and re-reading what George Orwell wrote 50 years ago on the political prostitution of the English language.

"In minor violence . . . the incident rates were equal for men and women. In severe violence . . . more men were victimized than women."

Female Violence Against Men Is a Serious Problem

Philip W. Cook

Philip W. Cook maintains in the following viewpoint that although statistics on domestic violence focus on men's violence against women, women are just as likely to initiate or engage in violence against men. Furthermore, he adds, women are more likely to use knives, guns, or other weapons against men, thereby causing injuries that are frequently more severe in abused men than in battered women. Compounding matters, Cook asserts, is the fact that there is little help available to either battered men or their female abusers. Cook is a journalist and lecturer and the author of *Abused Men: The Hidden Side of Domestic Violence*.

As you read, consider the following questions:

1. According to a survey cited by Cook, how many men are victims of domestic violence compared to the number of female victims?
2. What factors inhibit men from leaving an abusive relationship, according to Cook?
3. What solutions does the author present for dealing with female violence against men?

"Things started out pretty good the first couple of years. Then, she slowly changed. She always had a temper, but then we got into some money problems, and it got worse. She would get mad, and it would escalate all out of proportion. She'd start hitting. She'd slap at my face, and then keep slapping and try to scratch me. I'd put up my arms, or just grab and hold her hands. I never hit her back. I was just taught that you never hit a woman."

Joe S. is one of forty male victims of domestic violence that I interviewed over a two-year period. Canadian researcher Lesley Gregorash and Dr. Malcolm George in England have interviewed a similar number of such men. This apparently represents the sum total of all such men who have been the subject of in-depth published interviews. Some common patterns of behavior by victims and abusers have emerged; perhaps the most striking is the similarity between female and male victims and their abusers. Of the differences, the biggest is one of public and personal perception. In most cases, male victims are stuck in a time warp; they find themselves in the same position women were in twenty years ago. Despite the overwhelming numbers of male victims of domestic abuse, their problem is viewed as of little consequence, or they are somehow seen to be at blame for it.

Male Abuse

With support from the National Institute of Mental Health, Murray Straus, Ph.D., and Richard Gelles, Ph.D., conducted a nationally representative survey from the Family Research Laboratory at the University of New Hampshire, of married and cohabiting couples regarding domestic violence. The results were first published in 1977, as was a book with co-author Suzanne Stienmetz Ph.D., in 1980. Straus and Gelles followed up the initial survey of more than two thousand couples, with a larger six-thousand-couple group in 1985. In minor violence (slap, spank, throw something, push, grab or shove) the incident rates were equal for men and women. In severe violence (kick, bite, hit with a fist, hit or try to hit with something, beat up the other, threaten with a knife or gun, use a knife or gun) more men were victimized than women. Projecting the surveys onto the national population of married couples, the results showed more than eight million couples a year engaging in some form of domestic violence, 1.8 million women victims of severe violence, and two million male victims of severe violence.

The figures for abused women are the most often quoted figures regarding domestic violence in support of funding and attention for the problem. Most often, the equal or greater number of male victims are simply ignored. If couples not currently living together were included, the figure would likely be higher. These totals come with a qualification that is rarely mentioned, however; the surveys asked only if a particular type of violence occurred at least once in the past year. Other studies indicate severe repeated "battering" attacks to be much less common. The familiar statement that a woman is beaten every 15 seconds comes from the Family Research Laboratory surveys, using two million severe attacks as a basis. This statement is often attributed to the FBI or Justice Department, who have referred to it in publications, but it is not their result. To accept the Family Research Laboratory results for women should mean having to accept the same sources for male victimization, and to accept the most recent results, which find that some things have stayed the same since the surveys began. Both men and women experience an equal level of domestic violence victimization, but in the most severe category the number of women being assaulted has declined, from two million to 1.8 million while the number of men assaulted has stayed at two million. This means that a woman is severely assaulted every 18 seconds by her mate, and a man is similarly assaulted every 15 seconds.

Mentioned much less often is what the Justice Department does in fact say about domestic violence in their National Crime Survey: they report a rate half that of the academic results. The Family Research Laboratory surveys are recognized, however, as being more accurate since they are based on a nationally representative sample, are not labeled a "crime" survey and cover a range of violent actions that the Justice Department survey neglects. The Family Research Laboratory results have been upheld by more than thirty other studies in the U.S., Canada and Great Britain. In fact, a review of published academic literature by Martin Fiebert, Ph.D. at the University of California Long Beach found 70 empirical studies, 15 review and/or analyses and 85 scholarly investigations which demonstrate that women are as physically aggressive, or more aggressive, than men in their relationships with their spouses or male partners.

Violence Is Mutual

Most domestic violence is mutual, and most wouldn't happen if there was not a history of such violence in the family of origin.

By their own admission in the sociological surveys, women hit first at about the same rate as men do. About half of all incidents of violence are one-sided: the rest is mutual combat. The woman who slaps or throws things greatly increases her chances of being hit in return. More importantly, the sons of violent parents have a rate of wife-beating 1000 percent greater than those of non-violent parents. The daughters of violent parents have a husband-beating rate 600 percent greater. Only about 10 percent of violent couples have a family history that was non-violent. Ignoring violent women, and concentrating solely on inhibiting violent men contributes to the cycle of violence for the next generation.

Certainly, a man slapping or shoving a woman is much more likely to inflict injury than a woman slapping or shoving a man. Since much more domestic violence falls into the "general violence" category there would be more injuries for women. An examination of 6,200 police and hospital reports by social scientist Maureen McLeod, however, found that men suffered severe injuries more often than women did in domestic encounters. Seventy-four percent of the men reported some injury, while injuries among women average 57 percent. When domestic violence falls into the "severe" category, women are more likely to use a weapon than men. In Dr. McLeod's study, 63 percent of the men faced a deadly weapon, while only 15 percent of the women did. Additionally, a report published by Barbara Morse of the Institute of Behavioral Science at the University of Colorado found that men sought medical care for domestic violence injuries at a slightly greater rate than did women. A report published in the "Annals of Emergency Medicine" at one inner-city ER found a slightly higher number of males than females seeking treatment for domestic violence injuries. Apparently, it's just a matter of style. Women probably suffer a greater amount of total injuries ranging from mild to serious because they are struck with the most ready instrument, the human hand, which will cause greater damage coming from a man than from a woman, but when it comes to serious injuries where weapons and object use come into play, the injury rate is about the same or perhaps greater for men. Stylistic differences aside, the result comes out about the same for their partners: injury and intimidation.

"Dear, how do you feel about women's clubs?"

While the numbers show that a woman is nearly twenty-five percent more likely to be killed by her mate than a husband killed by his wife, the rate is virtually equal for black couples.

Another argument for ignoring the true nature of most domestic violence is to claim that women have a much more difficult time than men do in leaving an abusive relationship. This doesn't hold up to scrutiny either; in fact, low-income women are more likely, not less likely, to leave an abusive relationship than are affluent women.

Indeed, if there are children men may be more likely to be inhibited against leaving an abusive relationship than women. Men do know one thing: their chances of getting custody of the children are not very good. Their chances of unblocked visitation with the children from a possibly vindictive and abusive spouse aren't very good either. Losing a relationship with one's own children, possibly forever, can certainly be considered as a big factor in a man staying in an abusive relationship.

Ridicule and Isolation

Men also face another factor that abused women today don't face as much—ridicule and isolation. Who can they talk to about their problem?

"The cops show up, and they think it's a big joke," Tim S. explained after his live-in girlfriend hit him in the head with a frying pan, which resulted in severe bleeding and a deep cut. "I never did tell anyone [of my friends and family] about all this while it was going on, because they would assume that I had done something to her, or that I deserved it. If there had been a crisis line for men in this situation I would have called it, to find out what to do, what the options were, how to stop it."

Not having any resources to turn to for help with their situation, no victim's advocates, no crisis lines, no support groups, no media recognition, no shelters, and a pervasive attitude that supports a macho "I can handle it . . . I must be the strong and responsible one" kind of response, further inhibits a man from leaving an abusive relationship, or even acknowledging it.

Even if a man seeks out a therapist for help, he is likely to find none, contends counselor Michael Thomas of Seattle, Washington. "In talking with other therapists, I find that they rarely even ask questions of their male clients about the possibility of the client being abused. I think a great many clinicians are still resistant to seeing certain types of female behavior as abusive. If the client can't talk about it, it becomes internalized, and it increases the danger of the men exploding in rage themselves, getting depressed or suicidal, withdrawing from relationships, and other kinds of effects. I have also heard from female abusers who can't get help. There are very few resources out there, for either victim or abuser."

Challenges in Helping the Abused Man

Due to this lack of resources, the employee assistance professional faces unusual challenges in assessment and referral for the abused man. As Dr. George found out in England, it is probably best not to even use the term "abused husband" with employees, but the more neutral "victim of marital violence." Almost all of the presentations one would find for a female victim of domestic violence are present in the male, with these additional factors:

• Self-protective humor. Males will more likely use this to cover up the extent of injuries, and to disguise the matter as of no consequence.

• Males will use the "I can handle it" excuse to a perhaps greater extent, and treat any episode, even one resulting in injury, as no worse than what has happened to them on a playing field. The assistance professional will want to encourage a view that accepts the seriousness of physical and verbal abuse in an intimate relationship. Validation that there are many males who experience domestic abuse will help relieve the isolation the presenting employee likely feels.

• Males will use their view of acceptance of "manly" responsibility as a reason to stay in the relationship, and to provide protection for any children.

• Males may more likely tend to use the excuse of extra time at work as an escape outlet from the abusive home.

Referrals for marriage or private counseling should be considered only after screening work is done to assess the counselor's willingness to accept males as possible primary victims of domestic violence.

Recognition of this possibility for individuals, therapists, the news media and many helping professionals will come slowly. It should come as no surprise that national surveys show a significant drop in public approval of a man slapping his wife under any circumstances, but no change at all in approval for a woman slapping her husband.

The point is not to excuse violence. It should not matter who started it, or what the provocation was. True self-defense is one matter; however, research clearly shows that in the overwhelming majority of domestic violence incidents, a direct threat to one's life is not involved. If we excuse violent acts by women by saying that they must have been provoked or were in response to violent acts by men, then that would put us in the position of accepting violent acts by men under the same circumstances. It does not reflect reality, either, as women themselves say that self-defense was not the reason for the overwhelming majority of attacks on their mates.

The solution for dealing with domestic violence on a realistic and factual basis does not necessarily mean a threat to funding for shelters or crisis lines as they currently exist. I don't believe we need a second set of funding for men's shelters. Rather, a change in attitude can accomplish the same goals. The Valley Oasis Shelter of Lancaster, California, for example, treats each call from those seeking help with dignity and respect, man or woman. It has a separate facility for men with children in need of shelter. The Kelso, Washington, Emergency Shelter also handles crisis calls from men, and has a male support worker, while not providing shelter services. There is no reason current crisis lines cannot serve both genders. A small but growing number of domestic violence crisis lines have obtained a newly available male victim brochure in an attempt to reach out to this under-served population. A big impediment to these small efforts, however, is the Federal Violence Against Women Act, which apparently prohibits funds from being used to serve male victims. A little creative thinking and configuration could provide actual shelter services for males and their children in many circumstances. These types of approaches are rare, and if a recent survey by the *Detroit News* in Michigan is of any guide, even crisis lines that claim to be gender-neutral and helpful to abused men in public statements, may not be in reality.

A Complex Problem

No program to combat domestic violence will be very effective, however, unless the true nature of such violence is recognized. We need to believe what women themselves report in surveys; they start a quarter of the violence, men start a quarter of the incidents, and the remaining half involve mutual violence.

Unless this fact is recognized, women seeking help for their anger problem, lesbians and gay men with partner problems, and heterosexual men who are being abused will continue to be discriminated against and told that their problem isn't real. The facts show otherwise; their problem is real and it affects millions of people.

For more than twenty years, we have been presented with only one part of the equation. Given the legal and societal history of discrimination and oppression against women in many areas, this was appropriate: it is not appropriate today. It has become an "us" against "them" battle. The reality of domestic violence, however, tells us that it is more complex than that. Some cases can be attributed to mental illness, but most are due to family upbringing, poor self-esteem, alcohol abuse, and/or uncertain employment combined with low anger management and communication skills. Domestic violence is a human problem, not a gender problem.

If we fail to put resources and effort into dealing with the total reality of domestic violence instead of just one part of this phenomena, we only encourage a group-against-group effect which is a disservice to everyone. The sociologists tell us that domestic violence at some level affects a significant minority of British, Canadian, and US couples. It is a criminal tragedy that must be dealt with on an economic, social, legal and spiritual level, but evidence of these human events should not encourage us to declare that the family is a bankrupt construct. If we can move forward to a better understanding of the benevolent and malevolent nature of each gender, we increase the opportunity for constructive rather than destructive relationships.

"If domestic violence against men were a big problem, 'we'd have a men's shelter on every corner with a golf course and valet parking.'"

The Seriousness of Female Violence Against Men Has Been Exaggerated

Christine Wicker

While no one refutes that some women do batter and abuse men, the extent and seriousness of the abuse is not as severe as some men's advocates claim, according to Christine Wicker in the following viewpoint. Men are physically stronger than women and are therefore able to inflict more damaging injuries than women can, she reports. Wicker adds that some women deliberately provoke men into assaulting them, while others attack men out of self-defense or in retaliation for earlier abuse. Men are much more likely to dominate women through violence than women are, she concludes. Wicker is a staff writer for the *Dallas Morning News*.

As you read, consider the following questions:
1. What three reasons does Wicker give to explain why men do not report that they are victims of domestic violence?
2. What percentage of men being treated for injuries in a Kansas City hospital had previous convictions for domestic violence, as cited by the author?
3. What is true battering, according to Cindy Dyer, and why does that preclude most men from being victims of domestic violence?

Reprinted, with permission, from "Men as Victims: Advocates, Police Differ on Extent to Which Males Suffer Abuse in Violent Relationships," by Christine Wicker, *Dallas Morning News*, September 6, 1998.

Jim says his former wife chased him around the yard with a butcher knife, threw plates of food in his direction and kicked him in the back one morning as he was shaving.

"I remember one night I was terrified. She was threatening to kill me and the kids. I didn't want to go to sleep," said the Dallas man, who asked that his real name not be used because he is afraid that his young son would be ridiculed.

He said he never hit his wife. "I tried to talk her down," said Jim. "I'm a social worker, and I never thought I was a victim of domestic violence. I never even put myself into the category of victim."

Jim's experience is far more common than most people believe, say men's rights activists. They say many men never mention intimate violence either because they aren't severely injured, don't think they'll be believed or are ashamed.

The advocates cite studies that show women, as often as men, hit, bite, scratch, shove or throw things at their intimate partners.

But police, prosecutors and academics agree that women are still the ones who suffer the vast majority of injuries from domestic violence.

And thereby hangs the controversy.

Murray Straus is the scholar most often cited by men's advocates on the subject. His 1975, 1985 and 1992 studies of American couples show females assaulting males 50 percent of the time—and often striking first.

His work has been widely criticized. But "it's not only my studies," said Dr. Straus, co-director of the Family Research Laboratory at the University of New Hampshire. "There are now more than a hundred studies that find the same thing.

"If you don't take into account the injury, if you don't take into account who feels dominated by whom" it's easy to believe that women are as menacing as men, said the sociology professor.

His work is used by people such as Arlington father's rights advocate Roy Getting to say that battered men need shelters of their own. "Men are not making enough of what's happening to them," said Mr. Getting, who says battered men do exist and hopes to open a shelter for them in Arlington.

Dr. Straus disagrees. "We don't need shelters for men," he said. They aren't being physically injured in the way women are, partly because women aren't strong enough and partly, he says, because women aren't as willing to hurt men.

Men who experience continual acts of violence by women "are serious victims in that that's a hell of a life to lead," he said.

Men's advocates say widespread violence against men goes unnoticed by police and emergency room doctors who are trained to look for domestic abuse against women only.

"I have not seen it," said Mesquite police detective R.D. Robinson. As many as 90 domestic assault complaints pass over his desk in a month, many filed by men, he said. But he wouldn't call those men battered. "The assault occurred but not a serious bodily assault," he said.

In a 1994 study of emergency room admissions sponsored by the U.S. Department of Justice, 37 percent of women reported being injured by their domestic partners compared to 4.5 percent of men. Some of those were gay people injured by same-sex partners.

"One of the worst cases of battered women syndrome I've ever seen was a man battered by another man," said Dallas County District Attorney Cindy Dyer.

Steve Storie, an investigator with the Dallas district attorney's family violence unit, said that if domestic violence against men were a big problem, "we'd have a men's shelter on every corner with a golf course and valet parking."

"I'll handle every case in the State of Texas of women who batter men on a continual basis. Just give them all to me, and I'll have plenty of time," said Mr. Storie, who was a police officer for 22 years.

"I can tell you this," he added. "I don't sit here fainting and crying over pictures of what women have done to men. It's the other way around."

Hardly anyone denies that men are sometimes serious victims of female violence. "Some of the most aggressive people I've seen in policing are females in bar fights," said Dallas police Sgt. C.I. Williams, who heads the Dallas family violence unit. "It's naive to think that doesn't happen in domestic situations."

On the other hand, he said, "When you look at crime statistics in general, men commit the vast majority of assaults, and there's no reason to think that's not true in families, too."

The picture is complicated by the issue of male pride.

"First the man has to admit to himself and then admit to an outsider that he's been assaulted and that's pretty tough for a man's ego to handle," said Mr. Getting.

Police say many men are quite willing to say that their wives and girlfriends hit them, but that their stories don't hold up.

"If Mary scratches you on the arm and you break her nose and blacken both her eyes, you're going to be guilty of assault," said Sgt. Williams.

Men's advocates say an increasing number of women are assaulting men as a way of luring them into violence.

"One thing that happens a lot is that women's divorce attorneys tell them that one way to assure you get custody is to provoke your partner to slap you or kick or assault you in some way. You file a protective order and there's no way he will get the kids," said therapist Stephen Finstein, mental health adviser for Fathers for Equal Rights.

Pat Keene, a lawyer who often deals with women seeking protective orders, calls that idea ludicrous.

"I would never never advise someone to provoke violence. It puts their lives in jeopardy. Once the violence starts you can't be sure the perpetrator won't turn around and hurt one of the children as well," she said.

The point that fathers' advocates want to make is that violence is a two-way street, said Ned Holstein, a physician who is president of Fathers and Families in Boston.

"Men living in fear and being controlled by violence is not much of problem," he said. "What is a problem is thousands of children having their fathers taken away because of an exaggerated and one-sided portrayal of domestic violence as being something only men do."

On the other side, many experts say women most often lash out in self-defense or retaliation for previous assaults.

When Dr. Robert Muelleman studied victims of domestic violence in an inner-city public hospital in Kansas City, he found that half the men who reported being injured by women had previous convictions for domestic violence.

L. Kevin Hamberger found that women who use violence against their partners are acting in self-defense or retaliation two-thirds of the time.

"Even some of the women who say, 'I use violence to control my partner,' are battered women . . . who decided, 'I'm not taking this. I'm paying him back,'" said Dr. Hamberger, professor of family and community medicine at the Medical College of Wisconsin in Milwaukee.

Police, shelter workers, emergency room doctors and family violence prosecutors agree with men's rights advocates that there are nonviolent men being physically injured by female partners.

When men's groups put out requests for Dallas-area battered men to come forward, numerous men responded.

Using Violence in Self-Defense

Most domestic violence is committed by men against women. According to the Department of Justice, women are victims of domestic violence eleven times more often than men. And although some sources suggest that women use violence against male intimates as frequently as men do against female partners, most evidence shows that the violence inflicted by men is much more severe. Women who use violence often do so to defend themselves against an abusive partner.

Maria Hong, *Family Abuse: A National Epidemic*, 1997.

Some said they were being emotionally, financially and legally abused but not beaten. Others called to say they knew men physically abused by women in dramatic and dangerous ways, but they could not supply details.

Half a dozen men told stories of various physical assaults.

"Would you call drawing blood abuse?" asked one man, who didn't give his name. His wife awakens him three or four times a week by digging her fingernails into him, he said.

Another man, who didn't want his name used, said his wife attacked him in the groin area. Both he and his former wife had filed for protective orders. She got hers. He didn't. Anti-male prejudice was to blame, he said.

Mr. Finstein located three men who he said were strong examples of abuse. But as he predicted, the men downplayed the idea that they were victims. One told of his wife pushing and shoving but said physical violence wasn't a big factor in the relationship.

"It was just dirty down, cruddy living," he said of life with his former wife.

Another man had multiple arrests for domestic violence. His wife hit him and otherwise provoked him into hitting her, he said.

"We both fought," he said, admitting that he bloodied her mouth and blacked her eyes. "To me it seemed like she was the one who started it . . . Physically she would get the worst of it, but then I would be the one sitting in jail."

A former drug abuser said his wife became physically violent when he started cleaning up his own life. "Abusers use guilt and shame to control you. Once they lose those weapons, it escalates. That's what happened to me," he said.

Dr. Muelleman thinks some of the violence among American couples is what he calls "mutual combat."

"He's no more an abuser than she is. At least, that's what the women tell me. They say, 'We just fight.' I'll ask, 'Do you feel controlled?' and she'll say, 'No.'"

True battering is about controlling another person's life, said Ms. Dyer, who heads a unit specifically devoted to domestic violence. Few men are being battered in that way and many women are, she said.

"There are many controlling women but they don't typically use force," she said. "They use emotional tools rather than physical threats."

Dr. Straus agrees that women don't often manage to dominate men through violence but does believe they use violence to gain control. He also believes "violence by women is a serious social problem that cannot be ignored."

The so-called harmless kicks and slaps women deliver "keep women at risk," said the professor.

"He's a slob. So she hits him and when she does, she establishes the principle that it's morally right to hit when someone does something you don't like. . . . The problem with that is that sooner or later it's going to be her turn to do something that he doesn't like. That's the nature of marriage, and she has unwittingly provided the justification for him hitting her," he said.

"The principle has to be that there's no hitting by anyone in this family."

> "If the 25 percent figure [of battered gay
> and lesbian partners] is correct, that's the
> same percentage estimated for women in
> heterosexual relationships."

Domestic Violence Is a Serious Problem for Gays

Steve Friess

Domestic violence is not just a problem for straight women, argues Steve Friess in the following viewpoint. Gays and lesbians are battered at about the same rate as heterosexual women, he asserts, but there are few, if any, services available to gay victims or abusers. The problem of gay domestic violence is compounded when the gay community itself refuses to accept the seriousness of the problem. Friess is a writer for the *Advocate*, a gay and lesbian newsmagazine.

As you read, consider the following questions:
1. According to Susan Holt, how many years behind the battered women's movement is the problem of gay domestic violence?
2. According to Friess, why are gay batterers not allowed to attend counseling groups for male abusers?
3. Who is one gay celebrity who spoke out about his abusive relationship, according to the author?

Reprinted, with permission, from "Domestic Violence Behind Closed Doors," by Steve Friess, *The Advocate*, December 9, 1997.

D ana walked into the only battered women's shelter in her Midwestern city with a bloody nose, bruises across her chest, and a couple of fingers as mangled as her spirit. A caseworker raced to her, first calling in a doctor to tend to her wounds and then leading her to a room where she could rest. "You're in a safe place now," the caseworker comforted. "You can relax."

Dana believed her and sank into a soft cot, falling asleep without even slipping under the covers. For three days she let her paranoia subside, letting down her guard to tell her caseworker of the daily abuse she suffered at the hands of her lesbian partner.

On the fourth day Dana ran out of the shelter screaming. She had walked into a common area to find, sitting casually on a couch, the woman who for two years slammed Dana's face against the kitchen counter whenever Dana came home a few minutes late. "I just got the hell out of there, got into my car, and drove 600 miles to my mother's in Chicago," says Dana, who doesn't want her last name used. "I later found out that [her partner] told them she was abused, and because she's a woman they just checked her in too."

No Refuge for Men

At least Dana had three days of peace. When Curt Rogers of Boston fled the torment of a lover who had restrained him for three hours and threatened his life, there was no place to turn. "A gay man cannot get into a shelter, period," says Rogers, who found hideouts with the help of coworkers in the weeks after he ran away. "A lesbian, depending on the shelter or her willingness to hide her sexuality, can go somewhere. The gay man is left hanging."

Neither gay men nor lesbians have good options, and gay groups around the nation don't seem eager to touch the issue, according to the second annual "Report on Lesbian, Gay, Bisexual, and Transgender Domestic Violence," published in October 1997 by the National Coalition of Anti-Violence Programs. The report's release gave the issue its greatest surge of publicity yet, prompting a spate of stories in the mainstream media that advocates hope will lead to a broader recognition that domestic violence doesn't happen just to straight women. "We are about 20 years behind the battered women's movement in terms of information and certainly in terms of the amount of resources available," says Susan Holt, project coordinator for domestic-violence programming at the Los Angeles Gay and Lesbian Center.

No shelters exist for men, though in San Francisco, Boston, and a few other cities, battered males can obtain hotel vouchers from domestic-violence agencies. None of the nation's 1,500 battered women's shelters are devoted to lesbians, although some have caseworkers who focus on lesbian clients. And most crisis hot-line operators answer the phone expecting traditional battered-women situations. "I called one of those once," Dana says, "but I hung up when the woman on the phone asked me if 'he' was still there or if I expected 'him' to come home soon."

Little Help Available for the Gay Abuser

If few services are available to the gay abuse survivor, even fewer exist for the batterer. In Boston a group for lesbian and bisexual abusers was formed this year by Emerge, the nation's oldest agency treating batterers, and the organization hopes to start one for gay male abusers in the next year. Emerge's clientele consists almost entirely of straight men court-ordered into therapy, something that judges rarely demand of gay or lesbian abusers. "They'll more often be self-referred or urged to do this by a therapist or partner," says clinical director Susan Cayouette.

Hundreds of male batterer groups meet across the nation, but Cayouette and others don't allow gay abusers to attend because they believe it creates a volatile situation among men already prone to violence. "What we found is that straight men have an added problem—that there's racism and homophobia there as well as the sexism that makes them abusive to women," says John Hokanson, community liaison and chief educator at End Violence Now, an Atlanta-based group offering support services for victims and education for perpetrators of same-sex domestic violence.

Little reliable data are available to measure how pervasive gay domestic violence is, but activists frequently refer to several unscientific surveys [since the mid-1980s] that claim that 25 percent of gay and lesbian partners are battered. The study by the antiviolence coalition cited 2,352 cases of abuse in 1996 in 12 U.S. cities, a vast undercounting but still the most the coalition has ever been able to document, says report coauthor Greg Merrill.

If the 25 percent figure is correct, that's the same percentage estimated for women in heterosexual relationships. Yet activists meet with widespread resistance when they push the issue among gay men and lesbians. "Many people have expressed to me a great deal of embarrassment that we've revealed this report to the mainstream media because we shouldn't be promoting negative information about us," says Merrill, director of client services at San Francisco's Community United Against Violence. "People just don't want to talk about it. Gay people feel immune to domestic violence the same way straight people in the beginning of the AIDS epidemic felt immune to HIV."

Instead gay men and lesbians focus on combating hate crimes or winning various legal rights. "You tend to say, 'OK, I'm going to go home to the person who knows I'm gay, and I want to believe it's a safe place,'" says Hokanson. "There are a lot of hate crimes, but then to come back to our own relationships and be bossed around or abused is something we don't want to talk about."

Battling the Myths

Unlike the way gays worked early on to involve heterosexuals in the AIDS crisis, heterosexuals aren't rushing to insist that domestic violence is also a gay concern. Rather, gay domestic-abuse activists actually spend time trying to convince society that gay domestic violence exists. They're also working to debunk the notion that people in same-sex relationships ought to be able to defend themselves. "The person who is contacted for help will often assume that this is a mutual battering situation, which is a myth," says Lynn Frost, a lesbian abuse survivor on staff with Little Rock, Ark.'s Women's Project, one of the reporting agencies for the study. "Because both persons are of the same sex, the counselor or volunteer assumes there is not a power issue involved."

Police officers often make the same assumptions, a key

reason gay men and lesbians rarely file domestic abuse reports. "I would never call the police, because police officers are notoriously not safe," says Connie Burk, executive director of Advocates for Abused and Battered Lesbians, based in Seattle. "Very often officers can't figure out who is the abuser, so survivors are arrested instead because they're bigger or more butch."

Violence Is Prevalent

The data that exists on gay men's domestic violence is scant. A 1996 study, done by the National Coalition of Anti-Violence Programs (the accuracy of which is yet unknown) cited 2,352 cases of gay and lesbian abuse in 12 U.S. cities. The study indicated that gays and lesbians are more likely to be the victims of domestic violence than anti-gay violence, but they rarely report the abuse. "Research found that domestic violence occurs in 25 to 33% of all same-sex relationships," says Greg Merrill, spokesperson for San Francisco's Community United Against Violence.

The survey was billed as an unscientific tabulation of 1,566 acts of violence in 1996 in Chicago, Columbus, Minneapolis, New York, San Diego and San Francisco. (New York City recorded the highest number of homosexual violence with 454 acts, followed by San Francisco, 347; San Diego, 330; Minneapolis, 243; Chicago, 129 and Columbus, Ohio, 63). "We understand this is a fairly rudimentary survey, but there is essentially no research in the area," says Merrill. "We're trying to use this as a starting point to show it's a problem and that we need to explore the issue further."

Doug Sadownick, *Genre*, November 1998.

It's Sgt. Norman Hill's job to fix that in Boston. Hill, the police department's liaison to the gay community, gives recruits a six-hour training program on gay issues, an hour of which is devoted to handling same-sex disputes. "I think the workshops are working, because I have had instances where people have walked up to me on the street to say, 'I had a problem with my significant other, and we had to call the police, and they were excellent.'" Such success heartens activists but remains rare, with many officers denying that ignorance of gay issues interferes with their work. Sgt. Ernest Whitten of the Little Rock Police Department's domestic-violence division bristled at the suggestion that his officers might need training on how to handle gay domestic abuse, insisting, "We deal with them all the same." And abuse survivor Rogers, who started Boston's Gay Men's Domestic Violence Project after leaving his abusive relationship, says some officers in other parts of Massachusetts dismiss his message: "Try going into a room with 16 police officers in uniform who don't want to hear your story. Then you have to explain your gay relationship to them and tell them how it went bad, knowing you're confirming their inner thoughts about how it was doomed."

Progress Is Slow

Progress on any front has been slow, primarily because few of the millions of dollars spent annually by state and federal agencies are earmarked for the gay-related component of the problem. "It burns me up that a gay man who is a victim of domestic violence is being denied services simply because he is a gay man," Rogers says. "We're talking about life-and-death services, protection from a batterer. Things will eventually change, but people are going to have to get angry, get noisy."

First, though, the community needs to be educated. Unlike the battered women's movement—which received a huge boost from the publicity surrounding the murder of O.J. Simpson's ex-wife amid allegations that Simpson had abused her—gay abuse survivors have few famous examples or national talk shows to mirror their plight. Olympic diving star Greg Louganis revealed intimate details of domestic abuse in his autobiography *Breaking the Surface* and on the speaking circuit, but advocates say even his efforts weren't enough to jar a reticent community into alarm.

Indeed, many gay men and lesbians prefer not to believe a problem exists, says Dana, the abuse survivor. In the year after she left her lover, she tried to describe her experiences to her new lesbian friends but found they didn't want to listen. The 36-year-old woman has retreated to writing about her trauma on America Online message boards and hoping that someday someone other than her therapist will believe her. "If that kind of thinking exists in our community," she muses, "how can we expect anyone else to care?"

> *"While somebody might write a book about [domestic violence in gay relationships] and present it as a grave social problem, I don't see how a choice these unfortunates make is any of my business or concern."*

Domestic Violence Among Gays Is Not Society's Problem

Mike Royko

Mike Royko argues in the following viewpoint that because gay men do not get pregnant and are able to financially support themselves, it should not be as difficult for them to leave an abusive relationship as it is for heterosexual women. Therefore, he contends, gay men who stay in violent relationships make a conscious choice to accept the abuse they receive. Consequently, society has no obligation or duty to help victims of gay domestic violence. Royko, a nationally syndicated columnist, died in 1997.

As you read, consider the following questions:
1. In Royko's opinion, what is an unexpected problem of gay marriage?
2. Why did Royko initially believe that domestic violence would not be a problem in gay relationships?
3. According to David Island and Patrick Letellier, what is the explanation for why people batter their partners?

It appears that the issue of same-sex marriage is going to be more far-reaching than simply John marrying Joe or Linda marrying Sally.

Once these marriages are legal and accepted, then society will be confronted with problems such as spousal abuse.

Less of a Burden

I quickly discovered this when I recently wrote that spousal abuse in two-male marriages might be less of a burden for the police than it is in the conventional male-female marriage.

That's because a well-conditioned man should be better equipped physically to defend himself against an abusive male spouse than is the average female victim.

I was immediately straightened out on that point.

John Olson, a Milwaukee man, wrote:

> I expect you'll be hearing from a lot of people on that column, but the point I want to most focus on is the way you trivialized domestic abuse among gay men. I'm no expert, but a while back, I learned that a close friend had been a victim of abuse by his partner, so I read up on the topic. There's a book called *Men Who Beat the Men Who Love Them*, by David Island and Patrick Letellier, that estimates some 500,000 gay men are victims of abuse each year. The authors' point is that batterers suffer from a mental disorder. This disorder is more common among men than women, but like many other conditions, occurs equally among gay and straight men—so yeah, it does happen among gay male couples. And as you say, men are indeed more likely to be embarrassed about reporting it—police are less likely to respond to it, but the victims are just as likely to be seriously hurt by it even if they may theoretically be better able to defend themselves. I will mail you a section of the book and hope that you will read it.

Thank you, but no. I doubt that I will read it.

Not My Concern

It isn't that I don't sympathize with anyone who is being kicked around. But I happen to be pro-choice in many areas of life.

By pro-choice, I mean that if a guy—or 500,000 guys—choose to live with mentally unhinged "partners" who beat them up, that is their choice.

While somebody might write a book about it and present it as a grave social problem, I don't see how a choice these unfortunates make is any of my business or concern.

It seems to me that if Bill lives with Joe, and Joe makes a practice of pummeling Bill, then Bill would have the good sense to just pack a suitcase and get the heck out of there.

Easy to Walk Away

It should be easier for a man to walk away from an abusive relationship than for a woman since men don't get pregnant and have babies.

Also, men have a better deal in the job market, while many abused female wives might not have worked in many years or possibly ever. Plus, it can be tough for a woman to find a job that also gives her time to spend with her children.

So if an abused man has no kids to take along and support, and if he can support himself, why would he stick around and wait for the next fat lip?

Gay Marriage Can Benefit Taxpayers

[Domestic violence cases take] the cops away from their more important duties of chasing down murderous fiends or keeping their eyes peeled for someone with a burned-out taillight.

But if and when gay men start getting married, their domestic disputes should take a different form.

Gay men, especially those who are young, are known to be devoted to physical fitness, working out at health clubs, pumping iron and wrestling with Nautilus machines to keep their abs and lats nice and ripply.

So in a domestic brawl that turns violent, it might be less likely that the police would be called. Two muscular guys, or even scrawny ones, ought to be able to duke it out on their own and not involve the cops and the courts.

Mike Royko, *Salt Lake Tribune*, December 8, 1996.

But if his love or dependency is so intense that he chooses to stick around, whose problem is his fat lip or bloody nose?

Not mine, not society's, and surely not the cops' or a judge's.

In such matters, it is the choice of the individual. And, as a pro-choice sort, I say that if Bill chooses to tolerate a relationship in which someone clobbers him, well, that is his choice and I respect it—so long as he is not my neighbor and doesn't scream for help or pound on my door at night.

Gay Marriage

But if what you say is true—that 500,000 gay men are beaten by their "partners" each year—then I hope they give careful thought to so serious a step as getting married.

There's a point in a relationship where a marriage counselor can't do much good if what a guy really needs is a bodyguard.

On the other hand, as a believer in individual choice, I have to concede that if a man decides that he is so deeply in love that it is worth the pain of being whopped regularly, it is his frayed hide.

As another pro-choice advocate once philosophically said: "Different thumps and bumps for different chumps."

And I suppose it might be unusual, but it would be practical for someone with a wedding coming up to have himself listed for wedding gifts at a place that teaches karate or sells Mace.

Periodical Bibliography

The following articles have been selected to supplement the diverse views presented in this chapter. Addresses are provided for periodicals not indexed in the *Readers' Guide to Periodical Literature*, the *Alternative Press Index*, the *Social Sciences Index*, or the *Index to Legal Periodicals and Books*.

Aging	"Opening the Door on Elder Abuse," no. 367, 1996.
Vera Anderson	"Read My Face," *Utne Reader*, September/ October 1997.
Patricia G. Barnes	"'It's Just a Quarrel'," *ABA Journal*, February 1998.
Malcom Boyd	"Why Home Is Not a Haven," *Modern Maturity*, January/ February 1997.
Canada and the World Backgrounder	"Going over the Edge," March 1997.
David Kocieniewski and Kevin Flynn	"New York Police Lag in Fighting Domestic Violence by Officers," *New York Times*, November 1, 1998.
George Lardner Jr.	"No Place to Hide," *Good Housekeeping*, October 1997.
John Leo	"Monday Night Political Football," *U.S. News & World Report*, January 8, 1996.
Robin Runge	"Double Jeopardy: Victims of Domestic Violence Face Twice the Abuse," *Human Rights*, Spring 1998.
Doug Sadownick	"When the Going Gets Rough," *Genre*, November 1998. Available from Box 18449, Anaheim, CA 92817-8449.
Sally L. Satel	"Feminist Numbers Game," *New York Times*, September 9, 1997.
Marcia Smith	"When Violence Strikes Home," *Nation*, June 30, 1997.
E. Assata Wright	"Not a Black and White Issue," *On the Issues*, Winter 1998.
Abigail Zuger	"A Fistful of Hostility Is Found in Women," *New York Times*, July 28, 1998.

What Factors Contribute to Domestic Violence?

Chapter Preface

When the first written report of spouse abuse appeared in England in the 1760s, family violence was initially perceived as a lower-class problem. Further research has discovered that domestic violence is especially prevalent among the poor. Murray Straus, a noted researcher and director of the Family Research Laboratory at the University of New Hampshire, wrote:

> for the ordinary violence in family life, the pushing, slapping, shoving, there's not much difference by socioeconomic status or race. But when you come to the more serious kinds of violence, then the lower the socioeconomic status, the higher the level of violence, by very large amounts.

Other research supports Straus's conclusions. Gerald Hotaling and David Sugarman looked at eleven studies of domestic violence and found that in nine of the studies, a low socioeconomic status was a significant risk factor for spousal abuse. According to Hotaling and Sugarman, there are two possible reasons for this conclusion. First, lower-class families are subjected to high levels of stress and are less able to cope with it due to low education and few economic resources. Second, families with a low socioeconomic status frequently hold values that accept and permit family violence.

Other researchers contend, however, that domestic violence is not strictly a lower-class problem. They assert that battered middle- and upper-income women are not as visible to researchers. For example, affluent women are able to use private doctors and clinics. Moreover, the abusers of middle- and upper-class women are frequently well-known and respected members of the community, and therefore the women feel an additional burden of guilt and shame for their abuse which they hide by keeping out of the public eye. Poorer women, on the other hand, are often more willing to take advantage of local battered women's shelters.

Although researchers do not agree on whether or not poverty causes family violence, they do agree that women of all socioeconomic levels are victims of spousal abuse. The authors in the following chapter discuss other factors that are believed to lead to domestic violence.

*"Just as high alcohol intake leads to
cirrhosis of the liver, brain damage,
and heart failure, so does high alcohol
intake lead to violence in the family."*

Alcohol Abuse Causes Domestic Violence

Jerry P. Flanzer

In the following viewpoint, Jerry P. Flanzer contends that alcohol abuse has a high correlation with cases of domestic violence. He maintains that most families with alcoholism problems also experience domestic violence, and argues that this is because the use or abuse of alcohol by a batterer can prompt an abusive encounter, can lower the abuser's inhibitions against becoming violent, and can permit the batterer to rationalize the abuse. Therefore, Flanzer contends, alcohol is responsible for causing domestic violence. Flanzer was the director of Recovery and Family Treatment, Inc., a substance abuse and mental health agency in Alexandria, Virginia, at the time this viewpoint was written. He is now a social science analyst for the National Institute on Drug Abuse/National Institutes of Health.

As you read, consider the following questions:
1. How do children who grow up in alcoholic homes resemble children who grow up in abusive homes, according to the author?
2. What three factors must be demonstrated to prove a causal relationship between alcoholism and domestic violence, as cited by Flanzer?

Excerpted from "Alcohol and Other Drugs Are Key Causal Agents of Violence," by Jerry P. Flanzer, in *Current Controversies on Family Violence*, edited by Richard J. Gelles and Donileen R. Loseke. Copyright ©1993 by Sage Publications, Inc. Reprinted by permission of Sage Publications, Inc.

A lcoholism causes family violence. Just as high alcohol intake leads to cirrhosis of the liver, brain damage, and heart failure, so does high alcohol intake lead to violence in the family. At first glance at this assertion, the reader may be in shock, even outraged. Certainly one knows of alcoholics who are not prone to be abusive in the family, and certainly one knows of violent families where alcohol does not appear to be in the picture. Nevertheless, I remind the reader that there are other causes for cirrhosis of the liver, brain damage, and heart failure—but alcohol is certainly high on the list. Similarly, I agree that family violence has other causes. However, alcoholism, in its varying forms, is very high on the list. . . .

A Prominent Risk Factor

Substance abuse, alcohol abuse in particular, frequently emerges as the prominent risk factor contributing to myriad family problems. Despite media attention, alcoholism (alcohol dependence and abuse) continues to account for the overwhelming majority of the substance abuse problems in the United States and, not surprisingly, remains the most frequently mentioned form of substance abuse contributing to family problems in general and family violence specifically. Although the folklore across centuries and cultures refers to the link between alcoholism and family violence in all its forms (child abuse and severe neglect, sibling abuse, spouse abuse, and elder abuse), social scientists have begun to investigate the link between alcoholism and family violence seriously only in the past few decades. The link is becoming clear, whether one refers to the actual occurrence of violence in the home or to the intergenerational and developmental consequences of living in a home with a family culture of alcoholism and violence. In this viewpoint I take the broad view of the intergenerational effect of alcoholism on family violence, going beyond the specific concern of the immediate effects of alcohol to the more general concern of long-term effects. Similarly, I take into account the alcohol intake of all family members, not just that of the perpetrator of the abuse. . . .

Repeated clinical observations of the behaviors of abusers

and their victims have led to a consensus among experts about the behavioral sets of the participants. Universally, all abusers, whether hitters or drinkers, project blame onto others: "It's not my fault"; "She deserves that." Universally, all perpetrators (alcoholics/abusers) tend to be jealous and possessive of targeted victims. The slightest suspicion of a spouse's relationship with another, for example, brings tirades and recriminations. Often, abusers expect children to behave as their parents, or expect spouses to take care of everything. These role expectations are impossible to meet. If one questions an abuser about a critical incident, one finds that he or she does not always remember the details and may even "black out" the incident altogether. Regardless, the abuser is not abusive all the time. In fact, he or she might otherwise be a model citizen.

Victims tend to be socially isolated, ashamed to show their physical and emotional scars, and unwilling to expose their plight to others. Part of this social isolation is caused by the victim's internalization of blame. The victim mistakenly agrees with the abuser—"I deserve it." Invariably, the victim believes strongly in family loyalty. Family secrets are guarded to an extreme; maintenance of family integrity is desired at all costs. The perpetrator's violent and alcoholic behavior blocks the development of intimacy and masks the abuser's frightening feelings of low self-esteem. These deleterious behaviors also block feelings of dependency and the extreme fear of being "swallowed up" that is linked to concerns of losing one's identity. The perpetrator maintains the illusion of superiority and control over his or her own life and that of the victim and, in so doing, actually creates the opposite effect.

All parties become more disoriented. At first, they must structure time to maintain functional family relationships. But they generally find themselves losing identity, through, first, the total enmeshment and then the total lack of involvement, or disengagement, with one another. Some families, having lived only with drinking and violence, have accepted this as the norm for family life, and even when they want to change, they do not know the truly "normal" ways to act. They pretend, and act as they have observed others to be. Thus, as is observed with crisis-prone individuals, they appear rigid and adhere strictly to authority.

Children growing up in violent homes evidence many of the same symptoms as children growing up in alcoholic homes. Clinicians have reported similar portraits among and between these two groups of children: emotional triangulations, secrets and isolation, stressed relationships, failing finances, and hopelessness. Children in alcoholic homes appear to have the same litany of maladaptive behaviors as child abuse victims, including juvenile delinquency, low self-esteem, suicide attempts, overrepresentation among clients of psychotherapists, sexual dysfunction, and marital difficulties.

Substance Abuse and Violence

Given the string of clinical similarities, one may wonder if we are dealing with the same population. Are these essentially the same families, looked at from a different angle, if you will? Could it be that one abuse is contributing to or causing the other? Or are these two abuses mutually exclusive, but only by chance frequently occur among the same families? Or are these two forms of abuse symptomatic of yet a third factor? I believe it is plausible that alcoholism and other addictive drugs may be a primary cause of violence in families.

I am aware, as is the reader, that there are many families in which alcoholism or some form of family violence appears to occur without the appearance of the other. Not all alcoholic families appear to include physical, sexual, or emotional abuse, and not all violence in families appears to be triggered by drinking or the taking of drugs. But with further exploration of the history of the family, I suggest that this mutually exclusive occurrence is rare and not the norm. So the question may be, How can it happen that family violence occurs without drinking or drug use? I maintain that the pattern of effects of alcoholism/drug abuse on increasing family violence emerges with clarity when one broadens the definition of *alcoholism and drug abuse*. If researchers would examine the periods and cycles of abuse, abstinence and withdrawal, cognitive and neurological damage to individual family members, the frequency of alcohol or other drug (AOD) use, and AOD effects on family interaction and development, they would see that they have missed the presence of AOD in the preponderance of their studies. In other words, alcoholism, or other substance dependence or abuse, may be more than a contributory factor to family violence, it may actually be one of the primary causes of violence in the family.

Proving a Causal Relationship

In trying to prove a causal relationship, three properties must be demonstrated:

1. *Association*: Proof of significant associations or correlations of the key variable must be shown. The researcher must show that the causal variables in the "symptom" produced variations in the dependent variable.
2. *Time:* A clear temporal relationship, wherein one factor precedes the other, must be shown. The researcher must show that the causal variable occurs before the dependent variable.
3. *Intervening variables:* An explanation of the relationship of intervening factors as catalysts or products must show that this causal system is not spurious—not the product of other variables.

Association

. . . Alcoholism and child abuse and neglect have been shown to appear together in a host of studies and clinical reviews. Studies of child-abusing families similarly have shown varying rates of alcoholism among family members.

These studies have used a variety of clinical and research methodologies. They also have been inconsistent as to their definitions of key variables, such as the actual definitions of the levels or degrees of child abuse and neglect, spouse abuse, and alcohol abuse and dependency. These differences make comparisons across studies and subsequent clinical reviews difficult. Still, the trends are evident. The correlations between alcohol and child abuse increase when we include the drinking patterns of all family members and not just those of the perpetrators. Samples of incestuous fathers have been shown to have a range of associations between alcoholism and incest of from 20–25 percent to 50 percent. Samples of perpetrators of physical abuse show a range of association between alcoholism and physical abuse of 23 percent to 42–65 percent. Positive correlations—the greater amount of alcohol abuse correlated with greater severity of child abuse and neglect—have been found in a DWI sample and in an adolescent abuse sample. Such associations might even be underestimates: Both of these studies also note that many of the most severe drinkers no longer have the opportunity to be perpetrators or victims, as they have lost their families. Evidence of a curvilinear relationship between levels of abuse exists. . . . Having an alcoholic father might be related to being a victim of sexual abuse by a significant other. This finding seems to "delink" alcoholism as a direct cause, allowing speculation about a "secondary" relationship, but it strengthens the argument that when alcoholism is present in a system it supports an abusive relationship.

Time

Two timing issues need to be addressed: First, was there any drinking *before, during,* or *instead of* the violence incident? Second, is there any pattern connecting drinking and abuse viewed over long periods of time?

Several researchers report timing variables that link drinking to the abusive event. For example, . . . 57 percent of the male abusers in [one] sample and 42 percent of the female abusers [were found] to have been intoxicated during the abusive incidents. [Other researchers] found 13 percent of their abusing sample to be intoxicated during the abusive events. In a study of adolescent abusing parents, I found nearly half to be drinking instead of hitting their children, and most of the others to be drinking after abusive events. The examination of the relationship between the two abuses over a long period of time helps us to realize that either a continuous or a delayed effect may be occurring over years within families, and timing may be different during different phases of the life cycle or between generations.

Many researchers have reported intergenerational findings, in which abused children grew up to be alcoholic adults. . . . Researchers also have found that being raised in alcoholic homes is related to becoming a perpetrator of child abuse. So, in these studies, one abuse appears to precede the other intergenerationally, thus supporting the broader definition of a relationship between alcohol and violence. . . .

Intervening Variables

Alcohol can instigate violence. Violent behavior results from a combination of the situation, the drug, and the individual's personality. Psychological disorders or reactions to environmental stressors may cause the aggressive behavior more than the actual physiological effects of the abused drugs. For the aggression-instigating condition, an imbibing individual may be physiologically unable to attend to the ambiguous cues and complexity of behaviors that normally mediate social behavior. This individual, who in effect has tunnel vision, sees only immediate and limited cues that in themselves might instigate aggressive behavior. In some cases, the individual's ability to distinguish between aggressive/instigating and aggressive/inhibiting cues becomes impaired, and the vulnerability to engage in aggressive behavior increases.

Domestic Violence and Alcoholism

Studies have shown that though domestic violence is universal, it is more prevalent in substance abusers. F. Hilberman and M. Munson found that 93 percent of the persons causing violence on their wives were alcoholics. Marvin E. Wolfgang reported that in his study, 67 percent of husbands who beat their wives were alcoholics. There is no doubt that there is a higher incidence of domestic violence among alcoholics and drug addicts. It is disturbing to note that more and more boys and girls are turning to alcohol and drugs. Thus drug abuse, tobacco and alcohol may become a permanent feature of modern society. There is an urgent need to study the factors which prompts young boys and girls to resort to these habits. Domestic violence could be substantially reduced if we can reduce substance abuse by our young boys and girls. This nefarious habit has destroyed the social fabric and disturbed normal human relationship.

R.V. Bhatt, *International Journal of Obstetrics and Gynecology*, December 1998.

Alcohol causes disinhibition that can lead to violence. Much of the literature suggests that alcohol reduces inhibitions, which results in a higher likelihood of aggressive behavior. An individual harboring intense underlying anger that has been contained by psychological defense mechanisms can become physically aggressive and intimidating as a result of the disinhibiting effects of alcohol. . . . The abused drugs act as disinhibitors of pent-up underlying anger. This disinhibition can cause the drinking or drug-abusing person to do things that he or she would not ordinarily do were he or she not abusing drugs or alcohol.

Alcohol destroys normal growth and development of the individual and the family system. . . . The alcohol-involved family life is skewed toward short-term stability at the expense of long-term growth. The family accommodates to the demands of alcoholism, and distortions occur that shape family growth and development. This restructuring of family life establishes a milieu that tolerates and accommodates to violence.

Alcohol may serve as a rationalization for violence, allowing the perpetrator to avoid taking responsibility for his or her actions. Intense drinking by the perpetrator or the victim (spouse) often leads to increased marital conflict, the drinking party's lack of responsibility, and other environmental (often employment or financial) stressors.

Alcohol alters brain functioning. The ingestion of alcohol over time results in the laceration of brain matter. The changes in the brain/neurotransmitter system as a result of drinking may be a causative agent in the relationship between alcohol and violent behavior, especially during periods of withdrawal. "Withdrawal syndrome" is the brain's reaction to the absence of alcohol. Withdrawal symptoms include increased irritability, quick temper, and anger. Being in a hyper-irritable state, the drinker does not need much stimulus to react with anger.

The Key Causative Agents

In the matter of alcohol and family violence, the case for causality rests on evidence of association, timing, and the presence of intervening variables. The high frequency of association is strengthened by the expansion of the definition to include clinical relationship over time. As researchers take more careful clinical histories, they find evidence of AOD involvement in families prior to their presentation as "violent families." At the present state of knowledge, the strongest case for the causative relationship between AOD and violence are the five intervening variables presented above.

Well-functioning persons have greater capacity for autonomy than do malfunctioning persons. Individuals living under the intense anxiety of double abuse are likely to be less autonomous, less differentiated, less able to process perceptions on an objective level, more enmeshed, and governed by their abusive relationships and perceptions. Thereby, they are also more at risk for the occurrence of any dysfunctional, invasive behaviors of others. Stated in other terms, they are vulnerable to accepting external others' (the predominant culture's) belief systems and norms, being less able to govern their behavior by their own internal, moral, and self-worth/integral beliefs. This may account for abusive behaviors surrounding drinking within the violent pervasive American culture, and for less provocative behavior surrounding drinking in more "depressed" and/or less violence-tolerating cultures. The violent perpetrator, stressed by AOD, is less likely to be able to manage anxiety in the external world and, supported by the external world's acceptance of violence, more likely to exacerbate his or her dysfunctional behavior. He or she will drink more *and* hit more. The "context"—the "culture"—is the catalyst, the condition in which the cause, alcoholism, operates. I contend that AOD intake, abuse, and dependency are key causative agents for violence in the family. Although this position is in opposition to current mainstream thinking, the clinical experience of many therapists, as well as the evidence presented here, certainly warrants further testing of this position.

The views expressed herein are the author's and do not necessarily reflect those of NIH or DHHS.

*"If disinhibition explained the relationship
between substance abuse and woman abuse,
we would expect batterers who were
substance abusers to be non-violent when
their substance use was terminated. . . .
This is not the case."*

Alcohol Abuse Does Not Cause Domestic Violence

Larry W. Bennett

Larry W. Bennett argues in the following viewpoint that although there is a link between alcohol abuse and domestic violence, substance abuse does not cause men to batter their wives. Other factors, such as a child's home environment and exposure to drugs and alcohol, the abuser's education and income levels, and a need to control other people's behavior, are more likely to increase the risk of abusive behavior than alcohol abuse, he contends. Due to the interlinking relationship between substance abuse and domestic violence, however, Bennett maintains that one problem cannot be treated without treating the other. Bennett, an assistant professor at the Jane Addams College of Social Work in Chicago, has written many articles about substance abuse and domestic violence.

As you read, consider the following questions:
1. What are the seven perspectives on drug and alcohol abuse and domestic violence, as cited by the author?
2. What percentage of men had been drinking alcohol at the time of domestic violence, as citede by Bennett?

Reprinted, with permission, from "Substance Abuse and Woman Abuse by Male Partners," by Larry W. Bennett, published at www.umn.edu/vawnet/substanc.htm, September 1997. (References in the original have been omitted in this reprint.)

S ubstance abuse and woman abuse are closely associated in the public's mind, so much so that many people believe the use of substances is a direct cause of woman abuse. Others view substance use as a risk factor which, while not a direct cause, may increase the frequency or severity of woman abuse. Still others believe substance abuse and woman abuse are separate issues, and any apparent relationship between them is illusory. Substance abuse, as used in this viewpoint, refers both to the abuse of alcohol or other drugs, and to dependency on alcohol or other drugs. While partner violence includes same-sex violence, this discussion of partner violence will be limited to abuse of women by their male partners or ex-partners, so the term woman abuse will be used throughout this viewpoint.

Perspectives on Substance Abuse and Woman Abuse

The relationship between substance abuse and woman abuse is by no means simple, but simple concepts are often used to explain it. The simplest concept, and the most commonly accepted, is that the chemical properties of a substance act on an element of the brain responsible for inhibiting violence. Since no such inhibition center has ever been located in the brain, the disinhibition model has been challenged by many experts. If disinhibition explained the relationship between substance abuse and woman abuse, we would expect batterers who were substance abusers to be non-violent when their substance use was terminated. Experience suggests this is not the case; abstinent and recovering substance abusers are well-represented in domestic violence courts and batterers' programs. The effect of substance abuse on men who abuse women, if one exists, is much more complicated than disinhibition theory allows. Other perspectives of the substance-violence relationship are briefly described below. In terms of woman abuse, substances and substance abuse may be viewed as:

(1) An excuse. In many societies, including ours, substance use has a role as a time out from responsibility during which the user can engage in exceptional behavior and later disavow the behavior as caused by the substance rather than the self. Some observers suggest batterers use substances first as a ve-

hicle, then as an excuse, for being controlling and violent.

(2) A cognitive disrupter. Drugs or alcohol may reduce the user's ability to perceive, integrate, and process information, increasing his risk for violence. Substance-induced disruption or distortion of thinking, in conjunction with other factors, increases the risk the user will interpret his partner's behavior as arbitrary, aggressive, abandoning, or overwhelming. Batterers may be more likely than non-batterers to misinterpret the actions of their partners in this manner, and substances enhance the misinterpretation.

(3) A power motive. Substance abuse and woman abuse may share common origins in a need to achieve personal power and control. David McClelland argues that the alcohol-aggression relationship is conditional upon individual power needs. Small quantities of a substance tend to increase a social user's sense of altruistic power, or the power to help others. A large quantity of a substance for social users, or any quantity of a substance for substance abusers, tends to increase the user's sense of personal power and domination over others rather than their altruistic power. This power-using relationship seems to be specific to men, and is reinforced by many cultures.

(4) Situational. Violence may occur during the process of obtaining and using substances. The situational relationship between substance abuse and woman abuse is particularly relevant when illegal drugs are involved. Procuring and trafficking drugs increases the opportunity for exposure to criminals, weapons, and violent sub-cultures. Conflict between intimate partners over whether, where, and when to use substances is not uncommon, nor is it uncommon that such conflict ends in woman abuse. A battered woman may use substances with her abuser in an attempt to manage his violence and increase her own safety, or she may be forced to use substances with her batterer.

(5) A chemical agent. Substance abuse may increase the risk for woman abuse through chemical actions on brain mechanisms linked to aggression. For example, alcohol has been found to increase the aggressive response of people with low levels of the neurotransmitter serotonin. Psychiatrists are experimenting with using serotonin-modifying medications

such as Prozac with some batterers. However, there is no evidence that batterers are "hard wired" for violence, nor that their socialization or choice-making processes are not operational when using substances.

(6) Partial to certain characteristics. Substance abuse may increase the risk for woman abuse only for those men with certain characteristics. For example, alcohol abuse increased the chances of woman abuse in those men who already approved of situational violence against women and were under socioeconomic hardship. In Kenneth Leonard's national study of 23-year-old men, heavy drinking was associated with woman abuse only for those men with high levels of hostility and low levels of marital satisfaction.

(7) Effective across generations. Substance abuse and woman abuse are learned through observation and practice, and are related over time. Parental substance abuse and parental woman abuse may impact the development of children, increasing the chances of a child growing up to be an abuser, a victim of abuse, and/or a substance abuser.

Discussions of risk factors and divergent perspectives on substance abuse and woman abuse concern some battered women's advocates. They fear these perspectives may shift the responsibility for woman abuse from the abuser to another factor, such as feelings about his family of origin, problem solving skills, or psychopathology. These factors could then be targeted for prevention or treatment, ignoring key issues of gender and power. This is a legitimate concern. However, none of the perspectives discussed above interfere with an understanding that woman abuse is a choice that men make in a society which supports men's power and control. These perspectives also suggest interventions which may help men remain engaged and cooperative, better utilize punishment and education, and ultimately choose non-violence.

Substance Abuse and Batterers

How frequently do substance use and woman abuse co-occur? Using data from the 1985 National Family Violence Survey, Glenda Kaufman Kantor found that, for episodes of man-to-woman abuse, 22 percent of the men and 10 percent of the women report they had been using alcohol at the time of the violence; in three out of four episodes of woman abuse, neither party was intoxicated. However, we must remember that substance use and substance abuse describe different situations. The Kaufman Kantor and Murray Straus study measured only whether the batterer or victim had been drinking at the time of the violence (use), not their drinking pattern or the cumulative effects of drinking (abuse).

Debunking the Disinhibition Theory

The belief that alcoholism causes domestic violence evolves from a lack of information about the nature of battering and from adherence to the "disinhibition theory." This theory suggests that the physiological effects of alcohol include a state of lowered inhibitions in which an individual can no longer control his behavior. Research conducted within the alcoholism field, however, suggests that the most significant determinant of behavior after drinking is not the physiological effect of the alcohol itself, but the expectation that individuals place on the drinking experience. When cultural norms and expectations about male behavior after drinking include boisterous or aggressive behaviors, for example, research shows that individual men are more likely to engage in such behaviors when under the influence than when sober.

Theresa M. Zubretsky and Karla M. Digirolama, in *Helping Battered Women: New Perspectives and Remedies*, Albert R. Roberts, ed., 1996.

The proportion of men in the U.S. who batter increases with the frequency they get drunk. For blue collar men, the proportion who have battered in the last year rises from a low of about 2 percent of men who never get drunk to about 40 percent of men who get drunk often. For white collar men, the rate climbs from about 2 percent of men who never get drunk to about 9 percent of men who get drunk often. At first glance, this study appears to support the public's perception that batterers are "drunken bums": that is, men are more likely to batter if they are poor or working class and if they are highly intoxicated. But the "drunken bum" perspective on woman abuse is erroneous for several reasons. First, Kantor and Straus point out that the relationship between substance abuse and woman abuse is strongest for those men who already think woman abuse is appropriate in certain situations. Second, even though the per capita rate of woman abuse is greater in lower socio-economic sectors of society, woman abuse is practiced in all social classes. Third, the amount of alcohol used prior to most episodes of intimate violence is far less than imagined. In Kai Pernanen's study of alcohol-related violence in Thunder Bay, Ontario, for example, the average amount of alcohol consumed prior to the violent episode was only a few drinks. This suggests that the act of drinking may be more related to woman abuse than the effect of the alcohol. Also, drug use other than alcohol is more strongly correlated to woman abuse than is alcohol.

Taken as a whole, studies establish a link between substance abuse and woman abuse, but not a direct link. Substance abuse increases the risk that men will batter their partners, although the substance per se is not the key factor. Studies suggest that other factors link men's substance abuse to violence against their partners. Among the most important of these factors are: (1) his growing up in a violent and substance-abusing family, (2) his low level of education and income, (3) his believing that violence against women is sometimes acceptable, (4) his believing that alcohol or drugs can make people violent, and (5) his desire for personal power. One commonly-held notion which the studies do not support is that men who batter are very intoxicated, and are therefore "out of control" when they batter. Despite the impairment in men's lives caused by alcohol and drugs, domestic violence remains a matter of choice, a "guided doing."

The incidence of substance abuse by batterers seen in criminal justice, mental health, or social service settings is well above 50 percent, substantially greater than the incidence of substance abuse by batterers in the general population. Ongoing research suggests that batterers may differ from one another in important ways, including their substance abuse patterns, the extent of their non-family violence, and their affective stability. While not yet definitive, this research suggests that there may be different "types" of batterers. This somewhat controversial position, if supported by further research, may suggest different approaches to intervention with different types of batterers, with their substance use pattern being a key component of the typology.

Substance Abuse and Battered Women

While men using alcohol is glamorized in male culture, the effect of alcohol on women is compounded by that same culture's negative attitudes about women drinking. There is evidence that women use substances differently than men. Compared to men, women are more likely to use substances to self-medicate mood and cope with trauma, and are less likely to use substances as an instrument of aggression. Growing up as a victim or an observer of violence increases the risk for substance abuse as an adult. Compared to women who do not abuse substances, substance abusing women have experienced a higher rate of violence as children, and continue to experience significantly more verbal and physical abuse as adults. Substance abusing women are more likely than non-substance abusers to live with men who are substance abusers, and they are more likely to use physical violence to retaliate for being battered, which in turn increases their risk of more serious injury. Substance abusing women may be less likely to have the social and financial means to escape from their batterer.

Historically, staff working with battered women have had little confidence in substance abuse treatment programs. Recently, more woman-specific programs have been initiated in recognition that women's substance abuse requires different approaches to treatment, although these programs are still rare, especially programs for women with children. Substance abuse by battered women is under-assessed by many victim's programs. The clash of feminist/empowerment and disease perspectives models, the language of recovery programs (e.g. codependency), and the debate over what intervention must occur in which sequence are barriers which must be transformed into vehicles of cooperation in order to help battered women who are substance abusers.

Recommendations

Both research and experience suggests that substance abuse is one of several important factors which increases the risk of woman abuse. Substance use may be affected by other risk factors (e.g. violence in the family of origin, belief in the aggression-increasing power of substances) and substance use may affect risk factors in the present (e.g. power motivation, cognitive and behavior skills, and the belief that violence against women is appropriate under certain circumstances). These risk factors are not only personal, but bear the imprint of society. Various perspectives have been offered to explain these complex relationships, but no single perspective can explain the relationship between substance abuse and woman abuse in all cases. Conversations between domestic violence advocates and substance abuse professionals, cross training, and careful research will help us choose which perspectives are best for the development of practice and programs.

We are in the very early stages of developing interventions and programs which target both substance abuse and woman abuse, but a few tentative recommendations follow from our current level of knowledge. First, when either substance abuse or woman abuse are encountered in practice, the chance of encountering the other is substantial. This suggests that assessment for both problems is indicated if either problem is detected, regardless of the setting. Second, since substance abuse and woman abuse have an important, yet indirect relationship, viewing one problem as symptomatic of the other is not useful. Both substance abuse and woman abuse should be regarded as primary problems, and reduction of one problem to the familiar language and interventions of the other problem is ill-advised. From the second recommendation flows a third. Since the relationship between substance abuse and woman abuse is complex, since both are primary problems, and since both have personal and social causes and manifestations, it follows that social agencies and institutions which address these co-existing problems must be capable of addressing and managing their complexity. Since this is usually beyond the pale of a single agency, service networks and coordinated community responses to both problems are essential.

> "*[Men] feel encouraged, and basically* entitled, *to control, beat up, rape and otherwise degrade women, simply* because they can.*"

Patriarchal Customs Cause Violence Against Women

Viviane Lerner

Violence against women affects women of all income and education levels and is a basic violation of their human rights, asserts Viviane Lerner in the following viewpoint. She argues that government and church doctrines have encouraged violence against women since ancient times as a means of controlling their behavior. Men have been trained to use aggression and violence to resolve conflicts, Lerner contends, and until the world learns the art of nonviolent conflict resolution, men will continue to use gender violence to oppress women. Lerner is a French translator and freelance writer in Hawaii.

As you read, consider the following questions:
1. What is the most common reason men give to explain why they killed their female partners, according to the National Victim Center?
2. What problems face an abused woman who decides to leave her batterer, in Lerner's view?
3. What solutions does Lerner propose to combat gender violence?

Reprinted, with permission, from "War on Women: A Viewpoint on Domestic Violence," by Viviane Lerner, *Off Our Backs*, April 1997. (Endnotes in the original have been omitted in this reprint.)

The United States loves to talk about human rights and point the finger at those barbarian countries around the world who practice torture and rape on a regular basis. Under the U.S. criminal laws, nobody has the right to torture another person. In the words of Eleanor Roosevelt, "Where, after all, do universal human rights begin? In small places, close to home. . . . Such are the places where every man, woman and child seeks equal justice, equal opportunity, equal dignity, without discrimination." Yet, in the U.S. alone, a woman is the victim of domestic violence every 12 seconds, and every day at least four women die at the hands of their spouse, boyfriend, or lover. According to the National Victim Center, "every year, domestic violence causes approximately 100,000 days of hospitalization, 28,700 emergency department visits and 39,000 physician visits. This violence costs the nation between $5 and $10 billion per year."

Who Is Battered?

Now and then, we hear—rather loudly—of battered men. Granted, *nobody* should be battered. But given that, according to recent statistics, 96 percent of the adult victims of domestic violence are women, domestic violence obviously is a women's plight.

Much has been said on the "profile" of the battered woman. Thanks to the O.J. Simpson case, even the media admitted what we already knew: battering is not per se a poor uneducated woman syndrome. Though poverty does compound the problem, wealthy men (such as Aristotle Onassis, for instance) have been known to beat up their girlfriends and/or spouses. So where does the idea originate that battered women are typically welfare recipients and from poor households? Well, the mass media certainly cannot be relied upon to publicize millionaires as women batterers, can they? Moreover, as increasing numbers of people are thrown into poverty (in majority women, as we know well enough), of course we are sure to find a large percentage of battered women among the poor!

Then comes another array of specious definitions. The battered woman is codependent, or promiscuous, or a bad wife and mother, in short she is asking for it! Even if any of those opinions were true, isn't freedom from bodily harm our birthright? Does not it extend to *all* people? Calling his wife a "slut" or a "bitch" does not give a man the right to hit or rape her, let alone send her to the hospital for repair! Yet, according to a National Victim Center report, "one recent study found that possessiveness, which included infidelity, fear of termination of the relationship, and sexual rivalry, was the most prevalent reason given by a male offender to kill his romantic partner. Female offenders killed much more often for self-defense than for any other reason."

One of the questions most often asked is "Why doesn't she leave, then?" Sometimes it is purely rhetorical, only aimed at justifying one's apathy (as in "she chooses to stay with her torturer, so it isn't my business to do anything about it"), but not always. Now, imagine *you* are a poor woman with two or three children who has decided to leave the home battlefield permanently (most likely with divorce in mind, further down the road). You may turn first to your family, friends and neighbors. As everyone (but the 10 percent wealthy) is hurt by an exploitative economy, they find themselves struggling hard enough as it is to stay afloat. If they are socially conscious, empathetic and generous, chances are that they already are stretched to the limit, they have more than their share of problems without supporting an extra family at home, and dealing on top of it, with an abusive man's periodical angry visits! How many relatives or friends do you personally know who you feel certain would welcome you in this situation? Besides, women do not necessarily feel safe with family or neighbors; neither do they feel free to impose on them, for a variety of reasons. So, when the streets are more crime-ridden every day and the home is another battlefield, where can you go for a modicum of safety?

Thanks to dedicated workers—mostly volunteers—we have battered women's shelters. Yet the number of battered women is increasing while the federal and state funding available for battered women and related services is not only grossly inadequate as it is—there are only about a thousand battered women's shelters in the whole country—but decreasing! So, you first have to find a shelter that is not already running at full capacity. Now, imagine you do find space in a shelter for temporary relief from your torturer. There you will be given free refuge and counseling; the shelter workers will try to find you a job (if you don't have one already, not all battered women are unemployed, though battering sure does not help promote job stability!) and they will provide all kinds of practical assistance, so that maybe, just maybe, you will get enough time and support there to be able to escape your batterer permanently. For instance, they will, if you so wish, help you secure a Temporary Restraining Order, which makes it easier for you to gain custody of your children. Well, before you finalize your escape, another difficult question comes up: will you or won't you take the children with you? If all goes well and you are able to turn a new leaf and file for divorce, would you rather deal with the charge of "kidnapping" your children or that of "abandoning" them? And where will you find decent child care as you struggle as a single mother to hold a job while raising your children?

She *Does* Leave

By the way, she *does* leave. That the battered women's shelters are so often full bears witness to this.

She has to be a brave soul, as this is the time when she stands the most chances to be killed by her abuser.

She leaves, with the full knowledge that, if she is not successful and cannot manage on her own, somehow (the odds are not good, in today's society), she may have to take to the streets or go back to the domestic battlefield, with an even more abusive husband—intent on retaliating and more convinced that he's all-powerful and can do to her whatever he pleases with impunity.

At a time when we are flooded with admonitions about Family and Family Values, we may well pause to wonder: what is this family they are talking about? If we go by the Walt Disney image of nuclear family perpetrated by the media, a family is a loving unit of well-off and well-educated people (namely a man, his wife and children) who live in fashionable surroundings and are expert in non-violent conflict resolution. Whom does this myth benefit?

Then we discover that it is not by accident that the loud

heralds of "family values" belong either to the Government or to the Church.

How did the concept of the traditional family begin?

The Romans designed a family as a legal structure to insure the transmission of property to the male heirs. Given that only a woman could ever know for sure who a child's father was, men had to control her as a progenitor, in order to pass on their property to their rightful descendants. R. Emerson Dobash and Russell Dobash write, "Control of wives was of the utmost importance to the Romans, and it was expected that this task be carried out by the husband in the privacy of his own home rather than become a public matter. . . . Roman husbands had the legal right to chastise, divorce or kill their wives for engaging in behavior that they engaged in themselves daily. . . . If she were caught tippling in the family wine cellar, attending public games without his permission, or walking outdoors with her face uncovered, she could be beaten." Thus began the concept of traditional family that we have inherited as a model, however amended since.

"You seldom see such traditional family values these days."

"Pepper . . . and Salt" from *The Wall Street Journal*. Reprinted by permission of Cartoon Features Syndicate.

As for the Church, its misogyny is well known. In 325, for instance, the ecumenical Council of Nicaea saw it fit to debate whether women had a soul. Aren't we lucky they finally decided we did? After this brilliant debate, should we be surprised to find the Church consistently on the opposite side of

75

women? In the 13th century, Saint Thomas Aquinas wrote, "Father and mother are loved as principles of our natural origin. Now the father is principle in a more excellent way than the mother, because he is the active principle, while the mother is a passive and material principle. Consequently, strictly speaking, the father is to be loved more." How is this for "family values"? Not that woman fared much better under Protestantism. Here comes Martin Luther himself: "Men have broad shoulders and narrow hips, and accordingly they possess intelligence. Women have narrow shoulders and broad hips. Women ought to stay at home; the way they were created indicates this, for they have broad hips and a fundament to sit upon, keep house and bear and raise children."

Until the turn of this century, it was perfectly legal for American husbands to beat their wives, in exchange for providing for them and controlling their behavior in the "privacy of their own home." Half the population was thus reduced to pleasing their masters and making babies (sons, hopefully). This ran through the entire fabric of society, whether rich or poor. Since Roman times, a woman has been a man's property.

When today's bureaucrats and church officials talk of "family values" and some—such as Presidential candidate Bob Dole—go as far as saying that the welfare system is responsible for domestic violence, we reach new heights in absurdity. Is the alternative to the welfare system the creation of myriad jobs for both men and women? If mothers are to be able to enjoy more opportunities to work outside of home, are we about to, at long last, witness the advent of adequate child care? If the answer to both questions is no, then the plan to "keep the family together" is based on more coercion and hence, more domestic violence, not less. Where do women, the traditional beasts of burden of this celebrated family, stand in this grand plan? And what about the children?

Now, how much has changed since the early 1900s? How eager are the police—or the law—to protect the woman before she becomes yet another *casualty* of that war called "domestic violence"? Besides, who is feeding pornography and prostitution, thus encouraging violence against women (shouldn't we have a pious thought for Rev. Jimmy Swaggart?). Men are, as always, trained for aggression. They feel encouraged, and basically *entitled*, to control, beat up, rape and otherwise degrade women, simply *because they can*.

First, we need many more battered women's shelters and related services. Granted, it does not address the root of the problem, but we definitely need emergency relief while we explore other avenues.

Yet patriarchy is a system that ultimately enslaves both men and women, even though women are its prime victims. It generates oppression, hence violence, and, though it certainly has the upper hand—and a heavy one at that—not all men subscribe to it. Another possibility thus could be that, instead of battered women getting out of their homes with their children and no economic support, men of greater consciousness would organize male shelters where batterers will be placed; there, they will be provided with counseling and a basic support system. And while they keep working outside, their wages will automatically be sent to their spouses or lovers and/or children.

It is also high time, given the increase in violence all around, that we all learn the art of non-violent conflict resolution. This kind of training is already provided in various places, and will, hopefully, become a part of every child's school curriculum from kindergarten onward. What if we started organizing dozens of non-violent conflict resolution meetings in all our communities? Would not it be fabulous if we had as many of them as we have, say, Alcoholics Anonymous meetings everywhere?

Men, by and large, are the moneymakers, the lawmakers, the policy makers. What can battered women realistically expect from a male-dominated society, when it appears that the key to ending domestic violence (as well as many of the social and environmental ills of our times) lies precisely in the demise of Testosterone Supremacy? Well, as a reminder of all the free labor men have taken for granted for so long, maybe we could replace Mother's Day with Women's Week. Every year for a week, women will go on strike: no sex, no housekeeping, no caretaking, no unpaid work for men. It may help them give up the notion that we were born to be used and abused for their own convenience.

"If [domestic violence] purely were a matter of patriarchal arrogance, why is domestic abuse a problem even among lesbians?"

Partriarchy Does Not Cause Violence Against Women

Mona Charen

In the following viewpoint, syndicated columnist Mona Charen reports that the feminist view of domestic violence—in which men are aggressive, violent batterers who abuse women as a means of controlling them—excludes women who batter. Studies have found that women are just as violent as men in abusive relationships, she asserts. Charen charges that the feminist response to domestic violence—arresting and mandating treatment for men only, and blaming domestic violence on a hatred of women—does little to help abusive couples change their behavior.

As you read, consider the following questions:
1. How is the feminist view of domestic violence similar to the feminist view of rape, according to Sally Satel?
2. Why is arresting the man in domestic violence cases sometimes the wrong action to take, according to the author?
3. How many women and men are victims of domestic violence each year, as cited by Charen?

The trouble with ideologues is their simplemindedness. Communists saw a world full of evil: Conniving capitalists arrayed against virtuous, long-suffering proletarians. Fascists saw the world divided between master and inferior races. Modern feminists see violent, aggressive, uncivilized men victimizing helpless, innocent, peace-loving women. It is the mark of small minds that they seek to eradicate nuance and complexity.

The fact that an idea is foolish, however, is no guarantee against its general approbation. Writing in the summer 1997 issue of the Virginia-based *Women's Quarterly*, Sally Satel assays the state of domestic-violence treatment and finds that the feminist understanding of the phenomenon has triumphed.

The Feminist View of Domestic Violence

The feminist view of domestic violence, she explains, is akin to the feminist view of rape—namely, that all men are potential batterers and that battery is an expression of patriarchal control. In a dozen states, including Massachusetts, Colorado, Florida, Washington and Texas (with a dozen more coming down the pike), guidelines for handling domestic-abuse cases specifically forbid couples counseling until and unless the man has undergone feminist indoctrination.

The man is seen by feminists as the problem in all domestic-violence situations. It is natural, if you already know who's at fault, to leave the woman out of counseling. To include her would amount to blaming the victim. Some of these therapies, by the way, are funded by the federal government under the Violence Against Women Act.

Like all ideologues, feminists are casual about mere facts. Feminists have floated falsehoods in service of their vision of domestic violence and, as Satel notes, they create "new bogus statistics faster than the experts can shoot them down." Some have become legendary, such as the claims that "more women have been killed by family members in the past five years than Americans were killed in Vietnam."

This is not to suggest that domestic violence is an invention. Alas, it is not. But there absolutely is no reason to believe that feminist approaches to the problem do any good. In fact, they may do real harm.

Women Are Violent, Too

Take "must-arrest" laws. Many jurisdictions now require police to arrest one member of the couple (almost always the
man) whenever there is a complaint of domestic abuse.

But while arresting the man may be the right thing to do
in some cases, others are less clear. Arrest can inflame a situation that might not have escalated. And women themselves are sometimes the initiators of violence. Indeed, according to several studies, women are as likely as men to
resort to violence.

Is it more often self-defense in the case of women? Not always. About 1.8 million females are victims of severe domestic violence each year. But so are 2.1 million men (men sometimes hurt other men in the home). Most violent situations
involve both parties. Researcher Murray Straus, analyzing

Domestic Violence and Lesbian Couples

Consider domestic aggression within lesbian couples. If feminists are right, shouldn't these matches be exempt from the
sex-driven power struggles that plague heterosexual couples?

Instead, according to Jeanie Morrow, director of the Lesbian
Domestic Violence Program at W.O.M.A.N., Inc. in San
Francisco, physical abuse between lesbian partners is at least
as serious a problem as it is among heterosexuals. The Battered Women's Justice Project in Minneapolis, a clearinghouse for statistics, confirms this. "Most evidence suggests
that lesbians and heterosexuals are comparably aggressive in
their relationships," said spokeswoman Susan Gibel.

Some survey studies have actually suggested a higher incidence of violence among lesbian partners, but it's impossible
to know for certain since there's no reliable baseline count of
lesbian couples in the population at large. According to Morrow, the lesbian community has been reluctant to acknowledge intimate violence within its ranks—after all, this would
endanger the all-purpose, battering-as-a-consequence-of-
male-privilege explanation. Morrow's program treats about
three hundred women a year but she wonders how many more
need help. Because they are "doubly closeted," as Morrow
puts it, women who are both gay and abused may be especially
reluctant to use services or report assaults to the police.

Sally L. Satel, *Women's Quarterly*, Summer 1997.

several studies, concludes that 25 to 30 percent of violent clashes between partners are the result of attacks by women.

The feminist assumption in cases of marital abuse is that all men are violent and irredeemably so. The advice of leading "experts" always is the same: Leave. But many women don't leave and they are not, Satel argues, all pathetic Hedda Nussbaums, caught in destructive chains they cannot escape. [Hedda Nussbaum, who was beaten for years by her live-in boyfriend, Joel Steinberg, failed to protect their illegally adopted daughter, Lisa, from his abuse. After a severe beating, Lisa died November 5, 1987, of a brain hemorrhage while her parents snorted cocaine.] Many recognize their own contributions to the problem. Others weigh the costs of denying their children a father.

If it purely were a matter of patriarchal arrogance, why is domestic abuse a problem even among lesbians?

Abusive husbands and wives need to learn how to control their behavior and communicate better with one another. It does not help to tell them that men are violent out of hatred for all women.

"By virtue of their fame, athletes are not held to the same standard of conduct expected of the public at large. Americans display an unusual willingness to overlook deviance when it involves beloved athletes."

Sports Culture Contributes to Domestic Violence

Jeff Benedict

According to Jeff Benedict in the following viewpoint, news reports of athletes committing crimes, especially crimes against women, are becoming more and more common. However, he asserts, participating in sports does not cause men to batter and sexually abuse women. Instead, the fame and idolatry surrounding college and professional athletes contributes to their deviant behavior, he argues. Benedict contends that when society and the sports establishment refuse to punish athletes for their criminal actions, the athletes believe they are above the law. Benedict, the former director of research at the Center for the Study of Sport in Society at Northeastern University, is the author of *Public Heroes, Private Felons: Athletes and Crimes Against Women*.

As you read, consider the following questions:
1. What are the two most commonly cited reasons for the mass exodus of teenagers to professional sports, as cited by Benedict?
2. According to Roger Headrick, why do so many young men have such a difficult time adjusting to life as professional athletes?

W ith athletes' diminishing sense of shame over their socially degenerate behavior has come a corresponding rise in the frequency of their arrest, particularly for crimes involving women. The link between athletes' unbridled sexual appetites and their crimes is most poignantly illustrated among the upper echelons of revenue-producing sports, both college and professional, which have recently experienced escalating rates of violence against women. The increasing severity of the crimes mandates that policies be put in place to reduce the frequency of so-called role models running afoul of the law. Violent assaults, rape, kidnapping, and crimes involving seamy sex, drugs, and weapons have become all too common in the ranks of celebrity athletes.

The Voices of Denial

But as the association between athletics and lawlessness has been coming into sharper focus, the voice of denial from some coaches and other sports apologists has reached a crescendo. "We frequently read about athletes and coaches who are in trouble with the law," said Richard Lapchick, columnist for the *Sporting News* and director of the Center for the Study of Sport in Society at Northeastern University. "There are few denials of that image. Many seem ready to believe the worst. . . . The cases of a notable—but not extraordinary—number of football and basketball players who have assaulted women [are a] . . . misconception. . . . I have not seen anything that convinces me there is something about playing or coaching sports that made them [players accused of crimes] bad and evil."

Merely "playing sports" does not, of course, cause people to commit violent crimes—an obvious conclusion that can be reached simply by considering the millions of individuals, young and old, who participate in amateur athletics. Athletics per se has no known relation to the perpetuation of criminal behavior. When famous athletes violate the law, their behavior is more a function of their fame and background than their athletic training. "Why do we put our kids in athletics?" asked Greg Garrison, who prosecuted the rape case against Mike Tyson. "To teach them teamwork, discipline, practice, sacrifice of the individual for the benefit of the whole, sportsmanship, and goal setting. If you want to get rich so you can have lots of broads, which is right where athletics goes nowadays, then we've missed the boat completely."

Denying Responsibility

"I'll think we've come around the corner when I drive around through the projects and I see the photograph of the local black neurosurgeon on the front of the kids' T-shirts supplanting Magic Johnson, whose greatest contribution is to be the spokesperson for AIDS. 'There's nothing wrong with it if he can get it.' Yet his own conduct and his own dirty behavior is what caught him and nobody wants to say that because it's Magic Johnson. That's where sports has come off the tracks as a vehicle to a greater good."

Repeated denials that lawlessness among revenue-producing athletes is on the rise only perpetuate the potential for further, more serious crimes. Consider that during 1995 and 1996, no fewer than nine college and professional athletes landed in court for homicide-related crimes, which resulted in the deaths of seven people, five of whom were women. In all nine cases, the accused denied responsibility for their actions. In all but three the athletes went free.

The Temptations of Stardom

Stardom, by nature, dulls adherence to social norms, luring athletes to overindulge in illicit temptations. The enticements available to rich, famous athletes can prove particularly irresistible to the growing number of players who come from socially and economically deprived environments. In 1996, an unprecedented forty-two underclassmen declared themselves eligible for the NBA draft, including three high school players who opted to skip college altogether. Two of the most commonly cited reasons for the mass exodus of these teenagers and twenty-year-olds to professional sports, without finishing—or even starting—college, were financial hardship and a desire to remove their single mothers from unsafe neighborhoods.

The roots of dysfunctional families, crime-overrun neighborhoods, and family violence are many. Underneath the glamorous image of professional sports lies a growing number of young men exposed to all three of these conditions. "That happens to be, more often than not, the world from which they [professional athletes] come," said Roger Headrick [former president of the Minnesota Vikings].

The Typical Professional Athlete

Nonetheless, sports leagues and corporate advertisers rely more and more on popular athletes to attract consumer dollars. Ironically, the tacit expectation that athletes serve as model citizens is being thrust on vulnerable young men whose backgrounds offer little or no preparation for exceptional public scrutiny. Headrick offered the following composite sketch of the current professional athlete.

"My description of a typical professional athlete is that at twelve years of age they are either bigger, faster, or stronger than the rest of their male classmates. The other males in the school really admire them, and they get a certain amount of prestige and recognition out of that. By ninth or tenth grade, they have all the girls because the girls get attracted to star athletes in the school. By their senior year in high school, they start traveling for Friday night games. They take off Friday and there is usually a test on Friday and they miss it. But on Monday, some girlfriend gives them the test. So they pass it on Monday afternoon or Tuesday. And they get through high school that way, with a lot of help.

"They get into college, they get tutors—paid for—because they have a scholarship. So the tutors get them through. And they get summer jobs from alumni. By the time they are juniors or seniors, they have agents running around, who will advance them money against a future contract so they can get cars and stereo equipment and anything they want. Assuming they are drafted pretty high, and even if they aren't drafted pretty high, the minimum salary in the NFL this year [1996] is $129,000. How many twenty-three-year-olds or twenty-two-year-olds get $129,000? All of a sudden, for the first time in their life, they're out there on their own. They've never had to negotiate, write checks for themselves, negotiate a lease on an apartment, buy furniture . . . and they think, 'Why don't you just give it to me? I'm part of [team name deleted]. Give me the furniture. Give me the apartment. Give me this. Give me that.'

"It's always been given to them for the first twenty-two years. Boy, that's a real change of environment. Some adjust, some never do. They are immature, not terribly well educated, may not be the smartest people in the world, but they are out there in the public eye and they say things and do things that [most people] wouldn't condone, because they are just not equipped."

Of course, this generalization is not applicable to all college and professional athletes, but it describes a growing number of the nation's most popular role models well enough. At a time when society is searching for legitimate heroes, the traditional credentials of heroism—courage, honesty, bravery, self-sacrifice—are being replaced by visibility, wealth, and fame. "Athletes are more visible in society today, and they make a lot of money," said one NFL executive. "They are the way to a better life for a large segment of our population—at least, they are perceived to be. You go into ninth grade in the city of Los Angeles and ask all the kids that are playing basketball, you'd probably get 75 to 90 percent who believe that they can make it into the NBA. Yet there probably aren't going to be more than one or two. But when you have 75 percent who *think* that they can make it to the NBA, that's the life you want, that's the hope and dream out of whatever reality is at that point in time. Athletes have to accept some responsibility as being different. They accept the money, I guarantee you that. So coming with the money comes some sense of responsibility."

Athletes Are Entertainers

Celebrity is a poor substitute for legitimate leadership, however. The fact is, athletes' primary function is to entertain—a priority that often comes at the expense of responsible citizenship and perpetuates a kind of ethical relativism. "Professional athletics has become such a megagod that it is sometimes unresponsive to the morals of a community," said Garrison. "Sometimes it just doesn't matter what a superstar does, it's okay."

By virtue of their fame, athletes are not held to the same standard of conduct expected of the public at large. Americans display an unusual willingness to overlook deviance when it involves beloved athletes. Seldom do spectators display sufficient moral resolve to resist the urge to patronize cultural idols, even when their behavior descends below that of common criminals. One social policy expert warned, "Once society loses its capacity to declare that some things are wrong per se, it finds itself forever building temporary defenses, drawing new lines but forever falling back and losing its nerve."

Condoning Lawlessness

With little or no resistance from paying customers, the sports industry continues to condone lawlessness by offering scholarships and million-dollar contracts to criminally convicted athletes. The case of Nebraska's troubled running back Lawrence Phillips, a wonderfully talented but deeply troubled young man, illustrates the problem. The following remarks, collected during the predraft analysis period, were made by owners, general managers, and coaches who were considering drafting Phillips.

"When you get someone as respected as Tom Osborne vouching for a player's character, you have to put a lot of stock in that," said John Butler, general manager of the Buffalo Bills. (Following Phillips's much publicized conviction for brutally attacking his ex-girlfriend, Osborne had personally written every NFL team to compliment the character of his star running back.)

"I don't think he's an angel, but I think he's OK," said one team official, who wishes to remain anonymous. "I can't believe that anybody in their right mind that knows anything about personnel would pass this guy up."

Said Baltimore Ravens owner Art Modell, "I was impressed with the young man. He's quiet, has a good sense of humor, a sculptured body, enormously strong looks, big shoulders. There's a resemblance to Mike Tyson."

One team scout candidly stated that Phillips's best attributes as a running back were that "he's angry and hungry."

Ultimately, Phillips was drafted by the St. Louis Rams, who awarded him a $5-million contract. "Everybody deserves a second chance, sometimes a third and a fourth," said Rams assistant coach Johnny Roland. "What Lawrence did had nothing to do with drugs. It was harassment. He didn't kill anyone. He didn't stab anyone."

Not an Isolated Case

Unfortunately, the Phillips case was not an isolated one, but rather part of a pattern. Consider that prior to drafting Phillips, the Rams had elected to retain the services of defensive back Darryl Henley, despite the fact that he was free on bond, awaiting trial on federal drug trafficking charges. Henley's legal problems had caused him to miss most of the prior season. The Rams' 1994 media guide noted, "[Henley] missed most of season with team-granted leave of absence for personal reasons."

Badly in need of defensive help, the Rams wasted no time in returning Henley to the playing field while he awaited trial. Thanks in part to the testimony of Rams cheerleader Tracy Ann Donoho, whom Henley had recruited to carry twenty-five pounds of cocaine from Los Angeles to Atlanta, he was convicted in March 1995. While in prison, Henley orchestrated a murder-for-hire plot to kill both Donoho and U.S. District Judge Gary Taylor, who sentenced him. To finance the murders, he attempted to set up a $1-million cross-country drug deal. In July 1996 Henley was accused of plotting the killings in a thirteen-count indictment. On October 16, 1996, he was convicted. On March 10, 1997, U.S. District Judge James Ideman sentenced Henley to forty-one years in prison. "If there is a guy who needs to be locked down 24 hours a day, it's Henley," said Ideman. "The defendant obviously is a complete and hardened criminal."

The day after Henley was convicted, a jury in San Antonio, Texas, convicted NBA player Alvin Robertson of a crime against his ex-girlfriend Sharon Raeford. Robertson was accused of kicking Raeford's door, taking her wallet, destroying property, slashing furniture, and attempting to torch her home. Months before the incident, when Robertson was offered a contract by the Toronto Raptors, the team's management had defended its decision to stand by him despite his prior convictions for violence against women. Soon after they signed Robertson, he was arrested for assaulting a woman in a Toronto hotel room. Later that year he was convicted of assaulting women in two separate incidents in Texas.

College Sports

The practice of embracing skilled athletes who are criminals is not unique to professional sports. In the month prior to Henley's and Robertson's convictions, a slew of college athletes appeared in courts around the nation to answer charges for second and third offenses. On September 13, 1996, Texas Christian University football player Ryan Tucker was preparing for a court hearing on his involvement, along with three other teammates, in the beating of another student. The victim, Bryan Boyd, had been jumped from behind by the four players, who rammed his head into a brick wall, then severely beat and kicked him in the head. Boyd was left with a swollen brain, a fractured skull, and facial paralysis.

Prior to Boyd's beating, Tucker had been charged with two other assaults, and had been arrested the previous year for public intoxication. But Tucker remained on the football team and on scholarship at Texas Christian while awaiting trial for Boyd's beating.

Also on September 13, Mississippi State University basketball star Marcus Bullard appeared in a Guilford, Mississippi, court, where he was sentenced to three years in prison for violating his probation on drug charges. Five months earlier Bullard had led his team to the NCAA Final Four. An exceptional athlete on a team that was competing for a national championship, Bullard was allowed to retain his scholarship, despite a prior conviction for possession of cocaine with intent to distribute. Then in August 1996, Bullard was arrested on campus for pistol-whipping another student. "The court, whatever they do decide, please take it easy on me," Bullard said at his sentencing. But Judge Robert Walker did not extend the lenient treatment afforded Bullard by his basketball coaches. "I don't feel sorry for you, Mr. Bullard," said Walker, "because I feel you've received more breaks than one person is entitled to."

Coaches' willingness to employ criminals perpetuates players' off-the-field problems, virtually assuring that trouble-prone players will become repeat offenders. Coaches defend such practices by insisting they are trying to do what is best for troubled players. In reality, ruthless, self-serving greed motivates them to legitimize the criminal actions of deviant players.

Periodical Bibliography

The following articles have been selected to supplement the diverse views presented in this chapter. Addresses are provided for periodicals not indexed in the *Readers' Guide to Periodical Literature*, the *Alternative Press Index*, the *Social Sciences Index*, or the *Index to Legal Periodicals and Books*.

Jeannine Amber   "Young and Abused," *Essence*, January 1997.

Malcolm Boyd   "When Home Is Not a Haven," *Modern Maturity*, January/February 1997.

Canada and the World Backgrounder   "Going Over the Edge," March 1997.

Angie Cannon   "Unhappily Ever After," *U.S. News & World Report*, August 30, 1999.

Todd W. Crosett et al.   "Male Student-Athletes and Violence Against Women," *Violence Against Women*, June 1996. Available from Sage Periodicals Press, 2455 Teller Rd., Thousand Oaks, CA 91320.

Jeffrey L. Edleson   "Children's Witnessing of Adult Domestic Violence," *Journal of Interpersonal Violence*, August 1999. Available from Sage Periodicals Press.

Marilyn Gardner   "When U.S., Newcomers' Values Clash," *Christian Science Monitor*, July 16, 1997.

Claudia Glenn Dowling   "Violence Lessons: Abusive Behavior Begins at Home," *Mother Jones*, July 1998.

Armen Keteyian   "Crime Season," *Sport*, October 1998.

Wendy McElroy   "A Feminist Defense of Pornography," *Free Inquiry*, Fall 1997. Available from PO Box 664, Amherst, NY 14226-0664.

Ann E. Menasche   "An Interview with Diana Russell: Violence, Pornography, and Woman-Hating," *Against the Current*, July/August 1997.

William Nack and Lester Munson   "Sports' Dirty Secret," *Sports Illustrated*, July 31, 1995.

Sally L. Satel   "It's Always His Fault," *Woman's Quarterly*, Summer 1997. Available from 2111 Wilson Blvd., Suite 550, Arlington, VA 22201-3057.

Nancy Updike   "Hitting the Wall," *Mother Jones*, May/June 1999.

CHAPTER 3

Do Legal Remedies Against Domestic Violence Work?

Chapter Preface

Domestic violence advocates applaud a law passed in 1996, known as the Lautenberg Amendment, that is designed to protect victims of domestic violence from armed abusers. The Lautenberg Amendment prohibits anyone convicted of a domestic violence misdemeanor from owning or possessing a handgun. Weapons are used in 30 percent of domestic violence incidents; with such a high portion of abusers being armed, Rosemary Dempsey, vice president of the National Organization for Women, asks, "How can we accept any . . . law that would allow abusers to have guns?"

Opponents of the amendment contend, however, that the law is unjust, and they have filed lawsuits challenging the constitutionality of the law. They cite other gun-control laws still in effect that permit members of the police and military who have been convicted of felony domestic violence charges to keep their weapons under an "official duty" exemption. However, the Lautenberg Amendment does not contain such an amendment. Many members of the police and armed forces are finding themselves out of a job because they can no longer carry a weapon. According to Kelly Overstreet Johnson, a Tennessee lawyer who has filed lawsuits against the amendment, "It unfairly treats people who pleaded guilty years ago and did not know that something like this could now suddenly take away their livelihood."

Domestic violence advocates respond by pointing to studies that have found domestic violence is prevalent in 40 percent of military and police families, as opposed to 10 percent of families in the general population. Eleanor Smeal, former president of NOW, has little sympathy for batterers who are now out of a job. "Victims of domestic violence should expect a sympathetic officer, not one who has committed domestic violence himself," she maintains.

The controversy surrounding the disarmament of domestic abusers is part of a larger argument about whether changes made in the legal system to protect victims of domestic violence are fair and effective. The viewpoints in the following chapter explore other legal remedies for domestic violence.

> "Tough new laws are one way to reduce domestic violence and sexual assaults. Nothing sends a clearer message to a wife-beater . . . than prosecuting and jailing other wife-beaters."

The Violence Against Women Act Can Reduce Domestic Violence

Bonnie J. Campbell

According to Bonnie J. Campbell in the following viewpoint, the Violence Against Women Act allows the federal government, rather than just the states, to prosecute some domestic violence cases, thus sending a clear message that violence against women is a serious crime. However, Campbell asserts, even the toughest laws will not stop domestic violence until all Americans change their attitudes about intimate abuse. Campbell, the former attorney general of Iowa, is the director of the Violence Against Women Office, which was established in 1995 to provide assistance to state and local agencies to reduce and prevent domestic violence and sexual assault.

As you read, consider the following questions:
1. Why was Christopher Bailey prosecuted under federal law instead of state law, according to Campbell?
2. Why are domestic violence cases difficult to prosecute?
3. According to Campbell, how should Americans respond to potential and actual acts of domestic violence?

Reprinted, with permission, from "Breaking the Silence on Domestic Violence," by Bonnie J. Campbell, *State Government News*, July 22, 1996.

I t started with an argument.
  On November 26, 1995, Christopher Bailey of St. Albans, West Virginia, finished the argument by beating his wife Sonya until she collapsed. Then he put her in the trunk of their compact car and drove for five days through West Virginia and Kentucky before taking her to an emergency room. Sonya Bailey suffered irreversible brain damage and remains in a permanent vegetative state.

Christopher Bailey was arrested in Kentucky, but local police dropped the charges, saying they couldn't document what had occurred in their jurisdiction. Under West Virginia law, he might have received less than a two year sentence for his brutal assault. But federal prosecutors had a new tool, the Violence Against Women Act, signed by President Clinton as part of the Crime Bill. Christopher Bailey was found guilty of kidnapping and violating the Violence Against Women Act. He will go to prison, perhaps for the rest of his life.

The Act provides tough penalties for anyone convicted of crossing state lines to assault a spouse or domestic partner, closing a legal gap that has hindered prosecution of batterers in the past. Tough new laws are one way to reduce domestic violence and sexual assaults. Nothing sends a clearer message to a wife-beater—and Justice Department statistics confirm that women are battered far more than men—than prosecuting and jailing other wife-beaters. New laws, however, are not the only answer.

Changing Views

Too many Americans, including some in the criminal justice system, continue to believe that domestic violence is a private matter between a couple, rather than a criminal offense that merits a strong and swift response. Traditionally, our society has upheld the belief that what occurs within a family's home is no one else's business. The public's attitude has been that family problems should stay in the family. Even today, the victim of a domestic assault runs the risk of being asked, "What did you do to make your husband angry?"

Thankfully, state legislators and governors are examining their laws to insure that those who commit "intimate" crimes are dealt with just as severely as those who commit crimes against strangers. All too often, penalties have not been severe, and a wife who has been repeatedly beaten could not expect her tormentor to be punished for his crimes. There is enormous work to be done throughout our country. While the federal government can, and will, play an important role, the responsibility for addressing the crisis we face in violence against women remains primarily at the state and local level.

The Justice Department recognizes that state governments, courts and law enforcement agencies are going to need help and guidance in developing procedures that will protect women. One problem, in particular, has been the difficulty in enforcing restraining orders issued in one state when a victim moves to a new location. The department is working with a broad coalition of legal and law enforcement agencies to suggest guidelines to insure that women will be protected wherever they choose to live.

President Clinton's Crime Bill is helping to do that. In addition to enforcing tough new penalties, the Justice Department is providing substantial federal resources to help states create a seamless response system to aid victims and deal with perpetrators of domestic crime and sexual assault. In June, 1996, 49 of the 50 states received initial grants to train police officers, hire additional prosecutors, develop more effective strategies to prevent violent crimes against women, and apply state-of-the-art technology to improve their data collection and tracking systems.

These grants are a down payment on a major, historic federal commitment to assist states and communities in the fight against domestic violence and sexual assaults. By 2001, a total of $800 million in federal funds is scheduled to help states restructure their law enforcement response to address violent crimes which target women.

Our hope is that these federal funds will be used to promote a new dialogue among law enforcement officials, prosecutors, and victim service providers to create an integrated system addressing the needs of battered and sexually assaulted women. Grant money is available for police training programs, public education materials, and improved communication and data collection systems.

Training and technical assistance are critical elements in an effective effort to combat domestic violence. Police in communities across the country know how dangerous domestic violence can be. They empathize with victims, but often lack the information and resources they need to refer victims to service providers and pursue criminal charges against batterers. Training programs can provide police with information on shelters in their area. With the application of advanced technology, law enforcement agencies can develop innovative tracking systems to provide immediate information on previous complaints, protection orders or arrests for abuse.

A Real Solution to a Serious Problem

When it comes to family violence, most police officers do not make arrests, most prosecutors do not press charges and most judges do not impose tough sentences—and the women and children at risk go unprotected. What was needed was a real solution to this real problem. It took many years of hearings, reports and courageous women who came forward to talk about their abuse to convince Congress that combating family violence and sexual assault should be a national priority. The fight for [the Violence Against Women Act] took shape as a nationwide educational process, bringing about a slow recognition of the nature and extent of family violence and violence against women and culminating in a national commitment to improve the nation's dismal response.

[The Violence Against Women Act (VAWA)] is helping to make this commitment a reality. The years of debate and ultimate passage of VAWA not only provided the resources necessary for action but also created a momentum. Already states have made significant strides in turning the act into action.

Joseph R. Biden Jr., *Insight*, May 27, 1996.

Violence Against Women grants can also be used to create specialized police and prosecution units to deal with domestic violence and sexual assault cases. Public officials know better than most Americans how difficult it can be for crime victims to navigate their way through the criminal justice system. By integrating the work of specially trained police officers, prosecutors and victim advocates working on individual cases, these units can ensure that the victims of abuse receive the legal and emotional support they need from the time their abuser is arrested to the final disposition of the case.

New Approaches to Domestic Violence

The experiences in several cities, including Quincy, Massachusetts, and Seattle, Washington, indicate that innovations such as specialized domestic violence units can make a difference in crime rates. Congress understood the great challenge of developing intervention strategies that will work. They authorized funds for studies to provide the basic research we need to move forward. Several of those studies will be completed in the coming months, and the Justice Department will circulate them widely.

Just as importantly, we need to bring together professionals in a variety of professions—law enforcement, health, victim advocacy, education, business—to challenge them to work more effectively to protect victims and insure that perpetrators are punished. In the months since President Clinton appointed me to direct the Justice Department's Violence Against Women Office, I've travelled and worked with Joe Brann, the head of the President's police hiring program, to meet with local officials who are creating integrated approaches to combat domestic violence.

Our trips act as a catalyst to bring together men and women who serve on the front lines in this battle—police and prosecutors, community policing advocates, domestic violence experts, public health professionals, and community leaders. Only by working together in a cooperative effort can we insure that victims of violence don't fall through the cracks, and guarantee that perpetrators receive swift and sure punishment.

Even when cases are brought, domestic crimes are difficult to prosecute. All too often, the victims are so terrorized they fear for their lives if they call the police. More than once during my tenure as Iowa's Attorney General, I spoke with women who refused to press charges against abusers due to fear of being killed before the criminal justice system could act to save them. Their terror forced them to remain silent, despite the fact that silence is the batterer's best friend.

That is why all Americans have a responsibility to end the silence in our communities and change our attitudes toward domestic crime. Public officials can make a major difference by sponsoring town meetings, community forums and legislative hearings on the topic. People in our criminal justice system—police, prosecutors, judges, and, yes, even jurors—need to be educated about the role they can play in curbing acts of domestic violence.

Medical professionals who see the victims of violence need to report these crimes. Too often, doctors or emergency room personnel accept the statement of fearful victims that their bruises or cuts are the result of household accidents or falls. When a woman with a black eye says that she fell and hit the doorknob, doctors and nurses must ask: "Did someone hit you?"

We can't make our streets safe if we can't make our homes safe. Neighbors must contact the police when they hear violent fights in their neighborhoods. Don't turn up the television to block out the sounds of the drunken argument next door. Call the police. Teachers should be alert to signs that students have witnessed violence at home. Children who grow up in violent homes are more likely to become violent themselves.

Pastors and clergy need to become more involved as well. We just can't tell a battered spouse to "go home and make it work," as was done in the past. Sending a woman back to a battering husband often places her life at risk. Of course, we can't tell a woman who lives in a violent relationship what to do, but we can make a greater effort to let her know that other options are available for her and her children. Early intervention is crucial.

These crimes are serious. Tough laws and effective prosecutions, combined with education and a cooperative approach among law enforcement and social service agencies, will take time to be effective. Public officials must take the lead in raising awareness and increasing the resources needed for our efforts to be effective. It is too late for Sonya Bailey, but for millions of other women who live in abusive homes, our efforts to break the silence can make a difference.

> *"[The Violence Against Women Act] has boondoggle written all over it, which means that it will hurt taxpayers of both genders."*

The Violence Against Women Act Is Unjust

Frank S. Zepezauer

In the following viewpoint Frank S. Zepezauer argues that the Violence Against Women Act, a package of laws and programs designed to prevent domestic violence and provide protection to battered women and sexual assault victims, advances a feminist agenda that is unfair to men. Zepezauer asserts that men pay more taxes than women do to support programs that benefit only women. Furthermore, he contends, the act is unjust because more men are victims of crime than women, and many of those crimes are domestic violence crimes perpetuated by women against men. The best way to reduce domestic violence is to preserve the traditional family, he maintains. Zepezauer is secretary of the Men's Defense Association, a fathers' advocacy group.

As you read, consider the following questions:
1. How does Zepezauer describe "vintage gender feminism"?
2. How has the academic and economic status of men declined, according to Zepezauer?
3. In Thomas Sowell's view, where is the safest place for a woman?

Gender feminism translated into victim-rights newspeak gets attention where it counts—and costs—the most: in the mainstream media, state legislatures and Congress. Consequently, at a time when even Democrats support government downsizing, the . . . Violence Against Women Act, or VAWA, promises to drain $1.9 billion from the federal treasury. It is the mother of all wife-battering laws and it is a case study of the way such laws hurt men.

Feminist Assumptions

VAWA infuses big money into a vast network of female-specific government programs that amount to a feminist bureaucracy. It includes 260 women's commissions, 560 women's-studies programs and more than 1,000 domestic-violence and rape-crisis shelters. In Washington it includes a rabbit warren of agencies—most of them run by women, all of them for women and nearly all of them taxpayer funded.

Much of the money filters down to the states, which funnel millions every year into enforcement procedures and women's shelters. California, for example, spends more than $15 million a year. The sum increased 1,000 percent in just 12 months, the result of the media storm that blew in when the O.J. Simpson case broke. [Simpson, who admitted to battering his wife Nicole, was acquitted of her murder in 1995.]

With the Simpson case on every front page for months, wife battering escalated from a social problem to a national crisis, presumably afflicting "millions of households." And Simpson became Everyman. Columnist Anna Quindlen wrote that his was "the story of a man who, like many, many other men, beat up his wife and didn't think there was anything the least bit wrong with it." San Francisco journalist Joan Smith wrote that Simpson's spousal abuse is "woven into our culture." Mariah Burton Nelson, author of *The Games Men Play and the Women Who Get Beaten*, reported a society in which "hurtful acts are portrayed as natural—for men."

These heated declarations insinuated into prime-time discussion the feminist theory that violence against women—rape and wife beating—is how men maintain the satanic patriarchy. In Gloria Steinem's words, "Patriarchy *requires* violence or the subliminal threat of violence in order to maintain itself." This perception of the "patriarchy" is vintage gender feminism. It divides men and women into gender classes analogous to racial classes. From that perspective, all women form a victim class and in every intergender conflict men are the problem and changing them is the solution. This blinkered vision of victimhood places men as a privileged—and guilty—gender class beyond legitimate social concern.

The Declining Status of Men

All of which overlooks the steeply declining social and economic status of American men. Males are the minority of incoming college students. Compared with females, they earn lower grades, have more adjustment problems and show up more often on suspension, expulsion and drop-out records. They are falling behind girls in reading and writing and cluster heavily in remedial courses. They also engage more frequently in self-destructive behavior, racking up a suicide rate four times greater than girls. Christina Hoff Sommers, author of *Who Stole Feminism?*, calls boys "the educationally weaker gender" whose worsening academic and social performance deserves high-priority concern.

Relative to women, men have suffered a 25-year decline in average income and employment. In five business cycles between 1970 and 1993, jobs for men decreased while jobs for women increased. During the 1990–1992 recession, women gained 50,000 jobs while men lost 1.7 million. And since 1979, men without college education—usually in the lowest economic half of the income spread—have suffered a precipitous 17 percent drop in income.

Today, males 25–75 years of age have death rates from heart disease that are two to three times those experienced by females in the same age group. In fatal industrial accidents, men make up 94 percent of the casualties. Of all 15 of the leading causes of death in every age group, men have a higher casualty rate. And men die seven years earlier than women. Yet at the National Institutes of Health, women get twice as much gender-specific research money as men. Even so, in 1993, an Office of Research on Women's Health was established. It then won from Congress authorization for a $625 million research project on women's health problems.

The pattern is clear and disturbing. Government policy increasingly is implementing feminist assumptions about an oppressed gender class in special—and exclusive—need of tax money. The pattern is expensively reinforced by VAWA, which has feminist fingerprints all over it. Lawyers from the National Organization for Women were prominent in its formation and men's advocacy groups were shut out. Even radical feminist Andrea Dworkin testified before Congress, which is akin to consulting [Russian revolutionary] Leon Trotsky about a labor bill.

Making Sexism a Hate Crime

The result is codified gender feminism. At the heart of the act, for example, is a civil-rights provision that creates a federal remedy for violent crimes committed on the basis of "an animus based on the victim's gender." That makes any man-against-woman violence a potential hate crime. When the act was under consideration, civil-defense lawyer Andrew Good observed: "You face the prospect of a very intrusive investigation of your views. It's 'Are you or have you ever been a sexist?'"

The act provides $120 million for "pro-arrest grants" to encourage arrests in domestic-violence cases, which means more men arrested solely on the complaint of a woman. This provision has nasty potential. Men's-rights advocate Fred Hayward observed that, "Getting a restraining order is so easy that it has become a standard opening gambit for many women seeking favorable divorce settlements." It is even easier under VAWA.

Much of the $1.9 billion will finance a new task force as well as an army of counselors, trainers, consultants and coordinators, a classic example of bureaucratic inflation. It's no wonder that magazine editor Ruth Shalit called it an "alliance between feminist absolutism and patriarchal condescension." Good called it a "well-intentioned God-awful piece of legislation whose consequences only become apparent when it's too late to be repealed." It even left Dworkin wondering about the act's popularity. "The only possible explanation is that senators don't understand the meaning of the legislation they pass," she said.

VAWA therefore has boondoggle written all over it, which means that it will hurt taxpayers of both genders. But men pay most of the taxes and men still suffer most of the violence. They suffer it not only from a small minority of violent men but also, to a surprising extent, from women.

Female Complicity

Place "wife battering" in its larger context, that of "domestic violence," and one finds a high degree of female complicity. The term "domestic violence," for example, includes sister-against-brother violence, which is nearly as common as its counterpart. It includes abuse of the elderly, in which grandpas often are victims and daughters often are victimizers. It includes parental abuse in which 62 percent of the abusers are mothers and 62 percent of the victims are sons, many of whom are turned into potential victimizers.

And domestic violence includes spousal abuse in which "wives initiate and carry out physical assaults on their partners as often as men do," according to sociologist Murray A. Straus, who, along with coresearcher Richard J. Gelles, conducted studies in 1975 and 1985 reported in *Physical Violence in American Families*. They surveyed the yearly behavior of 2,143 married and cohabiting couples. Other studies had reported only the extreme violence that appeared on police blotters and feminist manifestoes. Straus and Gelles also asked wives and husbands separately about their violent behavior and then cross-checked results.

What wives admitted about their own behavior exposed a grim gender equality. At every level of violence wives delivered as well as they received. Wives, however, were six times more likely to suffer serious injury. This higher rate of female injury is emphasized by critics who otherwise downplay the Straus/Gelles figures. But other domestic-violence researchers have found parity even in this area. Susan Steinmetz, who worked with Straus and Gelles, reported that women are more likely than men to use injurious weapons. Sociologist M. McLeod came to a similar conclusion: "Violence against men is much more destructive than violence against women."

Straus, Gelles, Steinmetz and others have suffered abuse

from militant ideologues. But their work no longer stands alone. In 1993, Straus reported, "Every study among the more than 30 describing some type of sample that is not self-selective has found that the rate of assault by wives on male partners is about the same as the rate of assault on men by female partners."

Unjust and Paternalistic

The illogic of the notion that sexual crimes are inherently "gender-based" in the sense of bias against women is illustrated by the Iowa case of *Jane Doe v. the Rev. Gerald Hartz*, in which a woman claiming sexual abuse by a priest seeks damages under VAWA from him and the church. A month after the Hartz ruling, a Texas jury ordered the Roman Catholic Diocese of Dallas to pay $120 million to ten men who were molested by a priest as altar boys and to the family of a victim who had committed suicide. Is there any reason for female but not male plaintiffs in such cases to have access to federal courts?

The Women's Freedom Network also opposes VAWA because it perpetuates stereotypes of men as brutal aggressors and women as helpless victims. Women's lives have often been limited by paternalistic legal and social norms which held that women need special protection from life's dangers and that harm to women is worthy of more concern than harm to men. VAWA is little more than paternalism in a pseudo-feminist garb.

Cathy Young, *Women's Freedom Network Newsletter*, Summer 1997.

Other researchers have debunked the feminist belief that domestic violence is a "guy thing." A lengthening list of studies reveal that lesbian-partner battering is at least as common as its heterosexual counterpart. This data prompted social scientist Donald G. Dutton to conclude that "no direct relationship exists between patriarchy and wife assault."

Nor does any direct relationship exist between social reality and gender-feminist ideology. The reality is bad enough. Straus and Gelles report that about 1.8 million wives (1.4 percent of women) are assaulted severely every year, and 188,000 (0.14 percent) are injured. Those numbers reveal the anguish and anger pushing the domestic-violence movement. But they do not report an epidemic. And they do not report what is happening to men and boys. That their experience is seldom heard—much less accounted for—in gynocentric policies is just one more way that laws such as VAWA hurt men and women.

It also is one more way that Americans are distracted from our most serious social problem: father absence. Reduce that and we reduce domestic violence. As author Thomas Sowell argued in *The Vision of the Anointed*, the safest place for a woman is with a husband in an intact marriage. The safest place for children is in a home with a biological father. And the safest place for citizens—in the inner city and the suburbs—is in a neighborhood heavily populated with father-present households.

"Batterers see arrest as a punishment and punishment can deter battering behavior."

Mandatory Arrest Laws Can Reduce Domestic Violence

Julian Leigh

All states now allow police to arrest abusers for domestic violence offenses without a warrant and without witnessing the crime. Because the police are often reluctant to become involved in domestic violence cases, more than half the states now require law enforcement officers to arrest those accused by their partners of domestic violence. In the following viewpoint, Julian Leigh contends that these pro-arrest policies are more effective in reducing domestic violence than restraining orders or counseling the abuser or couple. However, she concludes, pro-arrest policies must be combined with consistent prosecution and sentencing policies to be most effective. Julian Leigh, MSW, is a researcher/educator for Domestic Violence Clearinghouse and Legal Hotline in Honolulu, Hawaii.

As you read, consider the following questions:

1. In what percentage of partner homicides have police been called out to the home at least once during the two years preceding the incident, as cited by Leigh?
2. How did the police respond to domestic violence calls during the 1970s, according to the author?
3. What reasons does Leigh give for why police do not arrest abusers?

Reprinted, with permission, from "Arresting Domestic Violence: Does It Work?" by Julian Leigh, published at www.stoptheviolence.org/news1.htm (1996).

Betty Jean Ashby

Betty Jean Ashby's life was in danger. She knew it. Her neighbors knew it. Louisville's Shepherd Square housing project knew it. Louisville police knew it. The man who was stalking Betty Ashby was Carl Branch, her common-law husband and the father of her four children.

When Carl showed up at her apartment on February 10, 1989, Betty climbed out a window, clad only in a shirt, and ran for her life. Carl, wielding an orange crowbar, pursued her across the street. He cornered her in the bedroom of a neighbor's apartment.

The neighbor, Marva Anderson, could only hug her four-year-old daughter and cry "Lord Jesus! Lord Jesus!" as Carl hit Betty in the head again and again until she sank to the floor, dead at age 22.

A police officer in her neighborhood had intervened on several occasions in what he called "domestic trouble runs." But the officer didn't arrest Carl then and kept no record of Betty's requests for help.

Penny Hall

On December 4, 1989, Penny Hall found herself lying in her mother's yard in Wheelwright, Floyd County. As she drifted back to consciousness, she remembers hearing her 10-year-old son crying, "Why did you hit my mommy and kill her, Daddy?"

Roger hadn't killed her; he had broken her jaw. And for a time, Penny entertained a fading hope that the law might redress her injury. The officer on the scene, Wheelwright Chief Terry Hill, said he couldn't make an arrest because he hadn't seen anything. He didn't bother to write a report on the incident either. On her own, Penny Hall swore out a warrant charging her husband with assault.

—Excerpts from journalist Maria Henson's Pulitzer Prize-winning editorials "To Have and To Harm," *Lexington Herald-Leader*, December, 1990.

Women Need Help

Had police arrested Carl Branch, would Betty Ashby still be alive? Should Officer Terry Hill have arrested Penny Hall's assailant at the scene of the crime?

In the United States, nine out of ten women murdered are

killed by men, half at the hands of a male partner. In 85 percent to 90 percent of partner homicides, police have been called to the home at least once during the two years preceding the incident. Fifty-four percent of the time, police have been called five times or more. These statistics suggest there are many more stories like Betty Ashby's.

Each year an estimated two to four million American women will be physically and/or sexually abused by their male partners. An estimated 30 percent to 66 percent of these women will call the police for help. . . .

Traditionally, police have been society's primary agent for domestic violence intervention. They offer victims protective powers and assistance when other service providers are not available. Police receive 85 percent of their domestic disturbance calls during evening, night and weekend hours and spend one-third of their time responding to those calls.

These statistics suggest many women, like Penny Hall, call for police to stop the violence of male partners. These statistics suggest police have an urgent opportunity to intervene in "domestic trouble runs." Can police help stop partner violence and save lives? If so, how? What is the most effective police response?

Police Response—Then

In the 1970's, society shifted its focus from changing the battered to changing the batterer. Andrew Von Hirsch noted a shift in the preference for rehabilitating batterers that predominated the 1960's and early 1970's to one that conceded available treatments had little or no effect. Police responding to domestic disturbance calls in the early '70's were encouraged to mediate the family violence—to act as crisis intervention counselors. State laws treated wife beating as a less serious offense, a misdemeanor. Only for felonies, more serious offenses, could an arrest be made without a warrant or without witnessing the alleged criminal conduct.

But during the late '70's and early '80's, several forces were converging to change the role of law enforcement officers. Feminists pressured the criminal justice system—insisting partner abuse be treated as a criminal offense.

Research of G. Marie Wilt and James D. Bannon published by the Police Foundation in 1977 linked police response to domestic violence homicides. In Detroit and Kansas City, police had been called repeatedly in a significant percentage of fatal "domestics." Victims were losing their lives and police departments were sustaining the high cost of multiple interventions.

In the famous Minneapolis Experiment, researchers compared police mediation, 24-hour stay-away orders and arrest interventions and concluded arresting most effectively reduced the likelihood of renewed violence. Despite significant limitations in the experimental design, the study was widely and well received.

Community Response

Mandatory arrest is just the first step of a coordinated community response to domestic violence whereby the abuser is arrested, charged, convicted, sentenced, and required to carry out the terms of the sentence. Arrest in coordination with other criminal justice efforts results in far more deterrence than arrest alone. Most abusers only get the message that abusive behavior is wrong and will not be tolerated if the message is consistently reinforced after every misdeed.

Joan Zorza, *Criminal Justice*, Fall 1995.

Lawsuits in the early 1980's also pressured police departments to change their policies—most notably the *Tracey Thurman et. al v. the City of Torrington, Connecticut* [case]. After being paralyzed from the neck down and permanently disfigured from stab wounds, Ms. Thurman was awarded 2.3 million dollars when police were held liable for negligence and the violation of her rights to equal protection under the law. Police had repeatedly failed to take reasonable action to protect Ms. Thurman from her husband's threats and violence.

In 1977, Oregon enacted the first statute in the country that required police to arrest abusers for misdemeanor domestic violence offenses, based on probable cause. By 1983, when the Minneapolis Experiment results were released, 33 states allowed police to use probable cause when arresting batterers—a presumptive arrest policy; and six states required police to arrest, at least in some assaults—a mandated arrest policy.

Police Response—Now

All states now allow police to arrest, without a warrant, without witnessing the crime, with probable cause. More than half of all states, and the District of Columbia, have mandated arrest laws. . . .

All across the country, . . . pro-arrest policies have dramatically impacted police response. In Connecticut arrests almost tripled, going from 7,000 the year before to 20,000 the year after the mandatory arrest policy was implemented. Arrests in Kansas City, Missouri, increased from 12–15 per day to 40–50 per day with the enactment of a new mandated arrest law. Iowa police officers were arresting at 20 percent of domestic disturbance calls in 1986, when the mandatory arrest policy went into effect, and were arresting 70 percent of the time by 1990. . . .

Today in the United States, legally, pro-arrest laws and policies—presumptive and mandated—are the official police response to domestic violence.

Why Arrest?

Arrest labels and identifies abuse and documents its pattern over time. Even when batterers are not prosecuted, arrest is often a first step for getting substance abuse and/or other treatment.

Another important rationale for pro-arrest policy is the goal of modifying the behavior of society. When police fail to arrest, prosecutors fail to prosecute and courts fail to convict, battering is tacitly condoned. According to J. David Hirschel et al.,

> Not to arrest may communicate to men that abuse is not serious and to women the message that they are on their own. It may communicate to children, who very often witness abuse of their mothers, that the abuse of women is tolerated, if not legitimated. It may communicate to the public at large that a level of violence which is unacceptable when inflicted by a stranger is acceptable when inflicted by an intimate.

Also, most pro-arrest policies establish battering as a crime against the state, relieving victims of the necessity to "press charges" against an abusive partner who may retaliate with more violence. In jurisdictions with mandated arrest and "no-drop" prosecution policies, cases are more likely to go to court with or without victim cooperation.

Law enforcement states the goals of pro-arrest police intervention are to stop the violence, protect the victim and carefully conduct a criminal investigation, charging perpetrators with the appropriate crime. Feminist policy analysis focuses on victim safety first. Thus, the question most often asked when evaluating pro-arrest policy effectiveness is: Does arrest deter batterers?

Does Arrest Deter Batterers?

Deterrence of violence is a primary short- and long-term goal of arrest policy, and specific deterrence theory relies on the belief that once an offender is punished, threats of future punishment will be more credible and violence will be inhibited. For arrest to work, the batterer must 1) have the capacity to control his behavior; 2) perceive arrest as a punishment; 3) believe he will be punished again.

There is a consensus among mental health and domestic violence professionals that partner abuse is learned behavior. Battering is a choice, not a psychopathology, and the majority of batterers will exhibit no severe psychiatric limitations. When evaluating pro-arrest policy as a deterrent, it is assumed most abusers do have the capacity to control their own behavior.

Next Kirk R. Williams and Richard Hawkins have argued that, theoretically, the act of arrest itself—with its shock value, the attendant label of "wife beater," and the fear of adverse publicity—is perceived as punishment by many abusers. Other batterers will perceive arrest as punishment because of the legal, rather than social, sanctions associated with being arrested, i.e., incarceration, fines, etc. Also, arrest as an act of punishment is most often administered immediately, enhancing its value as a deterrent. Results of the Minneapolis Experiment Replicate Studies tend to verify the suppositions that batterers see arrest as a punishment and punishment can deter battering behavior.

The Minneapolis Experiment tested and demonstrated the hypothesis that arrest is a better deterrent than mediating and short-term stay-away orders when police intervene in partner abuse. But the researchers did not test why arrest worked and later speculated the embarrassment of being arrested would be felt most by married and/or employed abusers because they had the most to lose. Two years after the original experiment, the National Institute of Justice funded six new studies in Omaha, Nebraska; Milwaukee, Wisconsin; Charlotte, North Carolina; Colorado Springs, Colorado; and Miami (Metro-Dade), Florida. Results from five studies have been published. Results from Atlanta, Georgia, were never made public.

These studies did not support the hypothesis that married men have more to lose than unmarried men if arrested, but did support the hypothesis that employed batterers are more likely to be deterred by arrest than unemployed ones. Findings show that arrest is the best deterrent for white and Hispanic abusers, regardless of their employment status, and that arrest deterred all employed abusers, regardless of race. Unemployed abusers, black and white, had higher recidivism rates and far higher rates of prior arrests.

Employed and unemployed batterers were not matched for other important variables, like criminal histories, substance abuse, etc.

Neither did experiments measure the impact of previous experiences with the criminal justice system. . . . The few studies that reported this information showed repeat offenders had very low rates of previous prosecution and conviction. Without subsequent negative consequences, the power of arrest to deter violence is undercut. . . .

Even though the Minneapolis Experiment and the replicate studies have serious inconsistencies and design flaws, this important work concludes mediation of family violence; short-term stay-away orders; and, of course, no response at all are not as effective as arrest in deterring individual batterers. This research also informs the criminal justice system and domestic violence service providers that unemployed batterers, especially those with criminal records, may be the most violent.

Unemployed batters, especially those with criminal records, may be the most violent. Offenders who are less invested in the social order, i.e., those without jobs, are less likely to be deterred by social sanctions. Arrest will, however, ideally serve to link these offenders to other more severe penalties.

Long-term, if enforcement is consistent, pro-arrest laws tend to establish more predictable, negative consequences for battering—an important social message. But it is difficult to measure both the long- and short-term effects of pro-arrest policy because the well documented reality is police do not consistently enforce the law. Despite a mandatory arrest policy, in 1986 Minneapolis police arrested at less than 20 percent of domestic disturbance calls. In 60 percent of the total 24,948 domestics, officers still mediated. Twelve percent of the time they did not respond at all; and about 6 percent of the time they did not complete the required written reports. . . .

Why Police Don't Arrest

Research shows a variety of factors influence police response, including who calls the police, who's present when police arrive, the offender's behavior, the officer's gender and attitudes about effective response. Police, when investigating all violent crimes, may operate from their own perception of when arrest should occur, i.e., commission of a felony, serious victim injury, use of a weapon, violence against the police and the likelihood of future violence.

Frequently laws change, increasing police responsibility without increasing funding for police departments. Inadequate staffing may negatively affect arrest rates. Pro-arrest and mandatory report writing laws expand an officer's workload. Not including court appearances, three to four officer hours may be required for each arrest.

Police may also become discouraged when their arrests repeatedly result in lack of prosecution. In one Ohio study only 24 percent, 256 out of 1,062 batterers arrested, were prosecuted and only 4 percent, 60 of the 1,062 batterers arrested spent time in jail. Seventy-five percent, or 1,408 of the 1,062 cases were dismissed because the victim requested this action or failed to appear in court. Even in jurisdictions with "no-drop" policies, which encourage prosecution despite lack of victim cooperation, prosecutors may screen cases based primarily on the victim's motivation to prosecute and whether or not she has a continuing relationship with her abuser. Likewise, police may selectively arrest based on victim cooperation. Lack of prosecution, multiple police interventions at the same household, and victim ambivalence may all be viewed by officers as evidence that their efforts are futile. . . .

Finally, officers may be reluctant to arrest when both parties are alleging violence. When they have difficulty determining the primary aggressor, rather than risk false arrest charges, officers may opt not to arrest at all.

An Effective Deterrent

The most current research reaffirms arrest is an effective deterrent to recidivism for many batterers and that those who do not respond to arrest are in critical need of more intrusive interventions. Unemployed batterers, who as a group have a higher rate of previous arrests, may be the most violent batterers. Arrest then becomes the first step toward conviction and incarceration of these repeat offenders.

Pro-arrest policies, presumptive and mandated, do prompt police to arrest more, if not all batterers. But, until arrest, prosecution and sentencing for battering [are] more consistent, deterrence theory suggests the potential for arrest to deter violence will not be fully realized. Batterers will continue to beat and terrorize their partners partially because they believe—they know—they will be permitted to do so.

Researcher/psychologist Lenore Walker cites the four most common beliefs of batterers:

Batterers believe . . .
I'm not doing anything wrong.
If I am, I won't get caught.
If I get caught, I can talk my way out of it.
If they "nail" me, I'll get off light.

Our challenge as a community is to make sure batterers' life experiences do not reinforce these beliefs.

*"Arrest may help some victims at the
expense of others and . . . may assist the
victim in the short term but facilitate
further violence in the long term."*

Mandatory Arrest Laws Are Unjust

Janell D. Schmidt and Lawrence W. Sherman

During the early 1980s, Janell D. Schmidt and Lawrence W.
Sherman studied the effect of mandatory arrest on domestic
abusers in Minneapolis and concluded that arrest was a deterrent. However, in the following viewpoint, Schmidt and
Sherman discuss the results of a duplicate study they per-
formed in 1992 in six cities. They argue that although
mandatory arrest does deter violence in some cases, it actually increases the risk of further episodes of violence in others. Since officials cannot know how a mandatory arrest policy will affect the residents of their cities, Schmidt and
Sherman recommend that mandatory arrest laws be repealed
and that police be allowed to arrest abusers at their discretion. Schmidt is the former director of the Crime Control
Institute office in Milwaukee. Sherman is the chair of the
criminal justice department at the University of Maryland.

As you read, consider the following questions:

1. What were the alternative police responses to mandatory
   arrest in the Minneapolis Experiment?
2. What is the single most consistent finding from the
   replication study concerning the effects of mandatory
   arrest on abusers, as cited by Schmidt and Sherman?

During the mid-1980s, widespread concern about the incidence and prevalence of domestic violence led many big-city police departments to radically change the way they policed a crime that affects millions of women each year. The often maligned "arrest as a last resort" tradition was replaced with written policies and state laws requiring arrest as the sole police recourse. Nationally, this enthusiastic shift generated a 70% increase from 1984 to 1989 in arrests for minor assaults, including domestic. Yet the movement to arrest batterers may be doing more harm than good. Research in six cities testing the "arrest works best" premise in deterring future assaults has produced complex and conflicting results. Police and policymakers are now faced with the dilemma that arrest may help some victims at the expense of others and that arrest may assist the victim in the short term but facilitate further violence in the long term.

The Minneapolis Experiment

The revolution in policing misdemeanor cases of domestic violence can be attributed in part to the 1984 publication of the Minneapolis Domestic Violence Experiment, the first controlled, randomized test of the effectiveness of arrest for any offense. Results from this endeavor found that arresting abusers cut in half the risk of future assaults against the same victim over a 6-month follow-up period. Alternative police responses tested were the traditional "send the suspect away for 8 hours" or "advise the couple to get help for their problems." The efficacy of each treatment was measured by interviews with victims and official records tracking the offense and arrest history of each suspect. Because arrest worked better than separating or advising couples, the authors recommended that states change laws prohibiting police from making warrantless arrests in misdemeanor domestic violence cases. They also advocated that replication studies be conducted to test the generalizability of the results in other cities with varying economic conditions and demographic complexions. But absent further research results, their recommendation to law enforcement was "to adopt arrest as the preferred policy for dealing with such cases, unless there were clearly stated reasons to do something else."

Although the authors opposed mandating arrest until further studies were completed, within 8 years legislatures in 15 states (including 1 in which a replication was currently being conducted) and the District of Columbia moved to enact laws requiring police to arrest in all probable cause incidents of domestic violence. This dramatic expansion of arrest practices has also been attributed to successful litigation against police departments who failed to arrest, to the recommendations of the 1984 Attorney General's Task Force on Domestic Violence, and to political pressure applied by women's advocacy groups.

It is not clear, however, how well these policies and laws have been followed or whether they have controlled repetitive acts of domestic assault. Observations of the Phoenix, Minneapolis, and Milwaukee police departments' compliance found that only Milwaukee officers consistently adhered to the policy. More important, the lack of labeling cases as domestic prior to policy changes renders attempts at before/after measures difficult. Further complicating evaluation or comparison efforts is the variable threshold for probable cause to arrest in incidents of domestic assault. In Wisconsin, only a complaint of pain is needed for police to effect an arrest; in Nebraska, visible injuries are required. Until 1989, Florida law required the parties to be married or formerly married in order for the incident to be considered domestic.

What is known about the impact of police arrest policies relative to domestic assault is that the vast bulk of cases brought to police attention involve lower-income and minority-group households. One reason may be a higher rate of domestic disputes among these groups; another may be a lack of alternatives short of police intervention that offer immediate relief. Although arresting thousands of unemployed, minority males each year may assist the goals of victim advocates and provide a brief respite for the victim, the skepticism of many police and criminologists relative to the deterrent power of arrest still remains. The key question of whether other police alternatives could prove more powerful or whether the police could be effective at all led the National Institute of Justice to fund replication studies in six major urban cities.

The Replication Studies

Beginning in 1986 and early 1987, police in Omaha (Nebraska), Milwaukee (Wisconsin), Charlotte (North Carolina), Metro-Dade County (Miami, Florida), Colorado Springs (Colorado), and Atlanta (Georgia) began controlled experiments to replicate the Minneapolis findings. Each site was afforded leeway to improve the methodology of the Minneapolis study and to design alternative nonarrest treatments to build on its theoretical foundation. Researchers in all the cities sought to obtain a sample size larger than the 314 cases analyzed in Minneapolis in order to test for interaction effects among the various treatments. In Metro-Dade, for example, a sample of 907 cases was obtained so researchers could compare arrest to no arrest, both with and without follow-up counseling by a specially trained police unit. In Colorado Springs, over 1,600 cases were used to contrast arrest and nonarrest with immediate professional counseling at police headquarters or the issuance of an emergency protection order. In Milwaukee, police provided 1,200 cases for the researchers to test the length of time in custody—a short 2-hour arrest versus arrest with an overnight stay in jail, compared to no arrest. The experimental team in Charlotte included a citation response along with arrest, mediation, or separation treatments in its 686-case sample. Only Omaha followed the Minneapolis design with 330 cases but added an offender-absent window of cases to test the effect of having police pursue an arrest warrant.

The results from five of these six later studies (results from Atlanta are not forthcoming) have clouded the issue for police and policymakers, although some victim advocates remain strident in their views that arrest works best. Perhaps most striking is that none of the innovative treatments, namely, counseling or protective orders, produced any improvement over arrest versus no arrest. The citation used to notify offenders to appear at a future court date in Charlotte caused more violence than an arrest. Only Omaha broke ground and found an effective innovation in its offender-absent experiment. Offenders who left the scene before police arrived and whose cases were randomly assigned to the warrant group produced less repeat violence than did similarly absent offenders assigned to the nonwarrant group. The issuance of a warrant may have acted as a "sword of Damocles" hanging over an offender's head.

In short, the new experiments reported both deterrent and backfiring effects of arrest. Arrest cured some abusers but made others worse; arrest eased the pain for victims of employed abusers but increased it for those intimate with unemployed partners; arrest assisted White and Hispanic victims but fell short of deterring further violence among Black victims. To understand these diverse findings and move toward a policy resolution, it is necessary first to focus on the effects of arrest compared to nonarrest as that is the central issue for police and policymakers concerned with determining the most effective or appropriate police response (see Table 1).

Table 1. Summary of Results of Six Arrest Experiments for Repeat Violence Against the Same Victim

Finding	Minneapolis	Omaha	Charlotte	Milwaukee	Colorado Springs	Miami
6-month deterrence, official measures	Yes	No	No	No	No	1 of 2
6-month deterrence, victim interviews	Yes	Border	No	No	Yes	Yes
6- to 12-month escalation, official interviews	No	Yes	Yes	Yes	No	No
6- to 12-month escalation, victim interviews	*	No	No	No	No	No
30- to 60-day deterrence official measures (any or same victim)	Yes	No	Border	Yes	No	1 of 2
30- to 60-day deterrence victim interviews	Yes	Border	No	Yes	*	Yes
Escalation effect for unemployed	*	Yes	*	Yes	Yes	*
Deterrence for employed	*	Yes	*	Yes	Yes	*

* = relationship not reported

Lawrence W. Sherman, Janell D. Schmidt, and Dennis P. Rogan, *Policing Domestic Violence: Experiments and Dilemmas*, 1992.

One central finding is that arrest increased domestic violence recidivism among suspects in Omaha, Charlotte, and Milwaukee. Although these three cities produced some evidence of a deterrent effect of arrest within the first 30 days, victims found that this protective shield quickly evaporated and they suffered an escalation of violence over a longer period of time. None of the follow-up measures produced the 6-month deterrent effect reported in Minneapolis. Some measures showed no difference in the recidivism of offenders arrested compared with those who police did not arrest.

Researchers in Colorado Springs and Metro-Dade found some support for the Minneapolis findings but only with limited measures. A narrow window of victim interview data (a 58% response rate in Colorado and 42% in Metro-Dade) confirms the deterrent power of arrest. But the less than ideal response rate might mean that victims who were interviewed were different from those who were not interviewed. Official records tracking recidivism in Colorado Springs did not uncover a deterrent effect of arrest, as some records did in Metro-Dade. Confounding the interpretation of the Colorado results was the fact that the vast majority of experimental cases (58%) were based on the offender's nonviolent harassing or menacing behavior toward the victim, perhaps distinct from the physical attack required to arrest for battery in the other cities.

Different Effects on Different Suspects

The different results from different measures in these cities suggests, then, that arrest has a different effect on suspects from different kinds of households. This finding is best summarized by the following statement by Lawrence W. Sherman et al.:

> Evidence that the effects of arrest vary by suspect comes from Milwaukee, Colorado Springs, and Omaha. In each of those cities, nonexperimental analyses of the official records data suggest that unemployed suspects become more violent if arrested, but that employed suspects do not. This consistent pattern supports a hypothesis that the effects of criminal punishment depend upon the suspect's "stakes in conformity," or how much he has to lose from the social consequences of arrest. Similar effects were found in Milwaukee for unmarried versus married suspects; unemployed, unmarried suspects experienced the greatest escalation of violence after arrest. The unemployment result is the single most consistent finding from the domestic violence experiments, and has not been contradicted in any of the analyses reported to date.

Are there other factors that could explain this varying effect of arrest on different suspects in different cities? A comparison of the data on prosecution rates, level of victim injury, number of married couples, unemployment rate, and ages of the suspects across all studies showed no consistent variation between the two groups of cities finding a deterrent or escalating effect of arrest. The only major difference was that a larger proportion of Black suspects was found in the "arrest backfires" cities (Omaha, Charlotte, and Milwaukee) compared to the "arrest deters" cities (Colorado Springs, Minneapolis, and Metro-Dade). But this pattern is not consistent, as one deterrent city (Metro-Dade) shared a similar rate of Black suspects with a backfiring city (Omaha)—42% and 43%, respectively.

Facts and Dilemmas

How carefully should policymakers and advocates tread through this maze of diverse findings? Applying these results to crime control strategies is complicated by the dilemmas and choices they present. Urban legislators and police chiefs in at least 35 states can choose between continuing the status quo and not mandating arrest, a choice that will continue to harm some victims. They can also legislate arrest, a choice that may harm victims presently served by a lack of policy. Choosing between the lesser of two evils is best guided by the following summary of the facts and dilemmas gleaned from the domestic violence research published to date:

1. *Arrest reduces domestic violence in some cities but increases it in others.* It is not clear from current research how officials in any city can know which effect arrest is likely to have in their city. Cities that do not adopt an arrest policy may pass up an opportunity to help victims of domestic violence. But cities that do adopt arrest policies—or have them imposed by state law—may catalyze more domestic violence than would otherwise occur. Either choice entails a possible moral wrong.

2. *Arrest reduces domestic violence among employed people but increases it among unemployed people.* Mandatory arrest policies may thus protect working-class women but cause greater harm to those who are poor. Conversely, not making arrests may hurt working women but reduce violence against economically poor women. Similar trade-offs may exist on the basis of race, marriage, education, and neighborhood. Thus

even in cities where arrest reduces domestic violence overall, as an unintended side effect it may increase violence against the poorest victims.

3. *Arrest reduces domestic violence in the short run but can increase it in the long run.* Three-hour arrests in Milwaukee reduced the 7% chance that a victim would be battered as soon as the police left to a 2% chance of being battered when the spouse returned from jail. But over the course of 1 year, those arrests doubled the rate of violence by the same suspects. No arrest means more danger to the victim now, whereas making an arrest may mean more danger of violence later for the same victim or for someone else.

4. *Police can predict which couples are most likely to suffer future violence, but our society values privacy too highly to encourage preventive action.* Largely because of the value our society attaches to privacy, especially marital and sexual privacy, no one has developed a recognized method, or even advice, for police to use in preventing domestic violence. A small group of chronically violent couples and incidents reported in apartment buildings produce most of the cases of domestic violence that police learn about, but the only policies now available react to the *incidents* rather than to the *patterns.* Ignoring those patterns allows violence to continue; addressing them requires methods that many Americans would call invasions of family privacy.

When Should Research Influence Policy?

Concomitant with these dilemmas is an even tougher question for officials charged with implementing effective policing strategies: Just how much research is enough to inform policy? The authors of the Minneapolis results were the target of much second-guessing and criticism from their colleagues over the reported findings and influence that the study enjoyed. Criminologists sought a more rigorous testing of the initial conclusions, perhaps foreseeing the risk of policy changes later proving to be unwise. Advocates, whose beliefs were validated by the results, and police policymakers, at least in Milwaukee, used the study to adopt arrest as the mandatory police response. In 1988, the Wisconsin legislature, perhaps less cautious than criminologists and motivated by ideological or politically pragmatic grounds, passed a law mandating arrest as the statewide response. This occurred despite their awareness of the ongoing replication in

Milwaukee testing the specific deterrent power of arrest. If a little medicine was good, a lot was even better.

The dilemma between limited research results and the need to do something about today's problems is also clearly illustrated by the Omaha offender-absent experiment. These findings may be far more compelling and relevant than the Minneapolis results because the offender is gone by the time police arrive in about half of the cases brought to police attention. Yet the study has had no observable influence on policy since its publication in an obscure journal. Modestly presented as a pilot study, no replications are being planned. Thus there is little risk that the findings will inform policy and later be contradicted. In the meantime, assaults on thousands of victims could conceivably be thwarted if prosecutors heeded the policy implications.

Sherman et al. posited that

> the replication dilemma thus also poses a choice between two wrongs. Both using and burying research results entail risks of harm. But as Americans become more sophisticated about the scientific process, they may come to expect revisions of policy based on new scientific evidence in this realm of knowledge as in others. Americans are accustomed to constant revisions of findings about diet and disease. Cholesterol, sugar, caffeine, alcohol, jogging . . . the "latest" evidence about their relations to health and longevity has changed significantly and repeatedly over the last twenty years, and many people and businesses have changed their behavior in response.

Policy Recommendations

To some, the choice between two wrongs invokes despair and inaction. Yet policing domestic violence may not be hopeless. Careful review of the policy implications, combined with the freedom to test alternative policies, can lead to more effective solutions. Use of the best information that Sherman et al. have to date guides the following five policy recommendations:

1. *Repeal mandatory arrest laws.* The most compelling implications of these findings is to challenge the wisdom of mandatory arrest. States and cities that have enacted such laws should repeal them, especially if they have substantial ghetto poverty populations with high unemployment rates.

These are the settings in which mandatory arrest policies are most likely to backfire. It remains possible but unlikely that mandatory arrest creates a general deterrent effect among the wider public not arrested. Even if it does, however, increased violence among unemployed persons who are arrested is a serious moral stain on the benefits of general deterrence. The argument that arrest expresses the moral outrage of the state also appears weak, if the price of that outrage is increased violence against some victims.

2. *Substitute structured police discretion.* Instead of mandating arrest in cases of misdemeanor domestic violence, state legislatures should mandate that each police agency develop its own list of approved options to be exercised at the discretion of the officer. Legislatures might also mandate one day of training each year to assure that discretion is fully informed by the latest research available. The options could include allowing victims to decide whether the assailant should be arrested, transporting victims to shelters, or taking the suspect to an alcohol detoxification center.

3. *Allow warrantless arrests.* Whereas mandatory arrest has become the major issue in some states, warrantless arrest remains an issue in others. Sixteen jurisdictions have adopted mandatory arrest laws, but at last report 9 others have still not given officers full arrest powers in misdemeanor domestic violence cases that they did not witness: Alabama, California, Michigan, Mississippi, Montana, Nebraska, New York, Vermont, and West Virginia. The success of arrest in some cities suggests that every state should add this option to the police tool kit. Deciding when to use it can then become a matter of police policy based on continuing research and clinical experience rather than the massive effort required to change state law.

4. *Encourage issuance of arrest warrants for absent offenders.* The landmark Omaha experiment suggests that more domestic violence could be prevented by this policy than by any offender-present policy. The kinds of people who flee the scene might be more deterrable than those who stay. A prosecutor willing to issue warrants and a police agency willing to serve them can capitalize on that greater deterrability. If the Omaha warrant experiment can be replicated in other cities—a very big if—then the warrant policy might actually deter more violence than do arrests of suspects who are still present. Because it will likely be years before more research on the question is done, such policies should be adopted now. They can easily be discarded later if they are found to be harmful or ineffective.

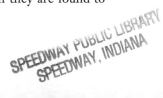

5. *Special units and policies should focus on chronically violent couples.* Because a limited number of couples produce most of the domestic violence incidents in any city, it makes little sense for police to treat all violent couples alike. It makes even less sense to frame the whole policy debate around responses to *incidents* when most of the problem is those chronic *couples.* The challenge is to develop procedures for violent couples that do not invade family privacy. Trial and error through research and development is required for any major breakthroughs. But an effective policy for dealing with chronic couples would have more impact than any other breakthrough. It deserves the highest priority in policing domestic violence.

A Frustrating Problem

The opposition to mandatory arrest laws presented here may frustrate or even anger many tireless advocates who have relentlessly grasped arrest as the preferred police response to incidents of domestic violence. To them, the suggestion that other institutions, such as battered women's shelters, treatment programs for victims and offenders, schools, and welfare agencies, may better serve victims is perhaps blasphemy. But they need not become too alarmed. However sensible that approach may be, the climate in many communities today is for law enforcement officials to get tough on crime. Regardless of the results of any scientific studies, the police will remain the primary institution coping with domestic violence among the poor and unemployed. This country's current fiscal crisis dooms any substantial investment in developing new programs in both the law enforcement and social service fields. The troublesome fact remains, however, that the punishment sought by advocates and community policymakers may encourage more crime.

"The majority of women . . . felt empowered by the protection order experience."

Restraining Orders May Empower Women Against Domestic Violence

K.J. Wilson

A restraining order, also known as a civil protection order, is a legal document issued by a judge that, in a domestic violence case, enjoins the abuser to stay away from his or her victim. In the following viewpoint, K.J. Wilson discusses the family court system and protection orders. Unfortunately, Wilson admits, civil protection orders are sometimes difficult to obtain and enforce. She adds, however, that obtaining a protection order gives many women a sense of empowerment and does prevent some women from being harassed by their abusers. Wilson is the director of training for SafePlace: A Domestic Violence and Sexual Assault Survival Center in Austin, Texas.

As you read, consider the following questions:
1. According to Wilson, how does the civil court differ from the criminal court?
2. What are the three legal strategies available to women to protect themselves against domestic violence, according to the author?
3. What are some limitations of protection orders, in Wilson's opinion?

The legal response to domestic violence consists of a complex network of processes, people, and laws. It has many different aspects, and a battered woman may become involved with any of them. Battered women are often implicitly expected to understand the legal system in order to access the help they need. That this system may seem intimidating and frightening is understandable considering that it often stumps the experts.

The Court System

The justice system is a framework comprised of law enforcement officers, prosecutors, and the court system. To better understand the system, it is helpful to understand the distinction between the *criminal process* and the *civil process*, as the differences between them can have a profound effect upon battered women.

The criminal justice system deals only with crimes. A crime is an act in violation of penal law. It is considered an injury to the state and will be prosecuted as such. The rationale for treating a crime as an injury to the peace of the state is to protect all citizens from a criminal who may strike again and thus must be deterred or punished. The result is that crimes can be prosecuted regardless of whether battered women take action. In fact, women are not always able to make the prosecution process work, such as in the case of murder.

The civil system deals with all the legal processes and matters that are not criminal. These matters include breach of contract, divorce, custody, property rights, recovery of money for injury, and a variety of other issues. In these cases, one party may sue another party. The legal remedy is usually an order by a judge. The judge can order the second party to do certain things or to pay money to the first party. It is important to remember that no one can be sent to jail as part of the remedy in the civil process except through contempt proceedings. Contempt proceedings more closely resemble criminal proceedings than civil and they may involve a jail sentence or a fine.

In most states women have a choice of three legal strategies to protect themselves against domestic violence:

1. Divorce or legal separation from the abusive husband

2. A civil protection order that requires the batterer to stop abusing, threatening, or harassing the woman
3. Criminal prosecution of the batterer

In appropriate situations women may be able to get both criminal enforcement and civil protection orders.

Civil Protection Orders

A civil protection order, now available in all fifty states and the District of Columbia, is an order issued by a civil court judge in response to a written petition from a battered woman. The order may command the abusive partner (a spouse, former spouse, or lover) to stop abusing, harassing, or threatening the woman and to stay away from her. The order can also provide for custody, supervised or unsupervised visitation, and child and spousal support; the abuser's eviction from the family home (even if it is held in the batterer's name); prohibition of the batterer from contacting the woman at her residence, school, or place of employment; payment for the woman's moving, medical, and legal expenses; and a requirement that the batterer get counseling or participate in a substance abuse or batterers' treatment program. If the protection order is violated, courts may hold the violator in contempt, impose fines, or incarcerate the violator, depending on state laws.

The remedies provided by protection order legislation are separate from and not replicated by existing divorce and separation procedures. Even if the woman plans to file for divorce, a civil protection order may be needed because her only recourse if the batterer violates the divorce conditions is to return to court to petition for a hearing. A violation of the civil protection order, however, would provide for his immediate arrest.

Civil protection orders are also distinct from criminal justice remedies. Other than in New York State, petitioning for a protection order does not prohibit a woman from bringing criminal charges against the offender at the same time. Some judges recommend that domestic violence survivors consider pursuing their cases both civilly and criminally, at least in cases involving aggravated assault and battery.

In cases involving ongoing criminal prosecution, protection orders may help prevent the opportunity for retaliation, intimidation, or undue influence on the woman. The criminal defendant in a family-based crime will often have both a strong sense of having been wronged and easier means to retaliate against the woman.

In addition, long-standing emotional ties and socialization factors can interfere with the criminal justice goals of punishing the offender and deterring future crime. These factors may influence a woman, leading her to withdraw as a prosecution witness. By prohibiting contact and evicting the batterer from the home, civil protection orders can often address the unique circumstances of criminal assault between intimate partners and thus increase the likelihood that the criminal prosecution will proceed.

Effects of Protection Orders

Before receiving a protection order, study participants experienced abuse ranging from intimidation to injury with a weapon. Researchers found that 37 percent of the women had been threatened or injured with a weapon; more than half had been beaten or choked; and 99 percent had been intimidated through threats, stalking, and harassment. More than 40 percent experienced severe physical abuse at least every few months, and nearly one-quarter had suffered abusive behavior for more than 5 years. . . .

The act of applying for a civil protection order was associated with helping participants to improve their sense of well-being. In the initial interviews, 72 percent of participants reported that their lives had improved. During follow up interviews, the proportion reporting life improvement increased to 85 percent, more than 90 percent reported feeling better about themselves, and 80 percent felt safer.

Susan L. Keilitz et al., *National Institute of Justice*, January 1998.

Many women, however, do not want the batterers charged criminally or jailed: they simply want the violence to stop. Other women are fearful of entering into an adversarial criminal procedure against their abusers. For these women, civil protection orders may offer the only form of legal protection.

In some states, a woman may ask the court for an order

herself, without the aid of a lawyer. This is called appearing pro se (meaning "for yourself"). In other states, an attorney must be present, whether a private attorney, a free legal services lawyer or representative from a law school clinic, or a government attorney.

Sometimes women may be able to get an immediate short-term emergency protection order, without the abuser being present, on the basis of their own testimony. This temporary order must then be served on the abusive partner and followed by a full court hearing, at which the batterer has an opportunity to appear, before it can be extended for a longer period. In some cases, it may take months to find and serve the batterer, hold a court hearing, and issue a longer-term protection order. These longer-term protection orders can be in effect for six months to two years.

Limitations of Protection Orders

In addition to their potential benefits, protection orders have historically had several limitations. Until recently, a woman who moved to another state to escape an abusive partner sometimes found that the second state could not enforce the restraining order issued in the first state. To receive protection, the woman had to obtain a protection order in the new state.

Another limitation is that it may be difficult for women to obtain an order. All states have mechanisms for issuing emergency protection orders and many have low filing fees, especially if the case involves a spouse or former spouse. In some situations, however, it may take several weeks for a woman to obtain a protection order, and the process sometimes involves prohibitively high lawyer fees and court costs.

Another factor to consider is that domestic violence frequently occurs during evenings or on weekends, when most courts are not in session. As of 1990, only twenty-three states provide for issuing emergency afterhours protection orders.

The utility of protection orders may also depend on whether they provide the requested relief in specific detail. Unfortunately, there are few guidelines for judges to use in interpreting the statutes and determining which types of relief are authorized and appropriate for individual women.

Not Always Enforced

In addition, civil protection orders have not always been consistently enforced. Few courts have developed guidelines or procedures for punishing violators. As a result, there remains a great deal of confusion in regard to arrest authority and appropriate sanctions for protection order violations. . . .

By the early 1990s, in forty states, a violation of a protection order constitutes either a misdemeanor or criminal contempt. In these jurisdictions, police may arrest an offender for a violation of any aspect of a protection order that the officer witnesses. Despite these statutory changes, however, enforcement remains procedurally complex for both police and courts. . . .

Positive Effects of Protection Orders

Despite these limitations, it appears that obtaining protection orders may have a positive impact on battered women's sense of personal control and self-confidence. Research surveying the experiences of seventy-five battered women using protective orders in Denton County, Texas, found that while women responding to the survey were generally very positive about the process of applying for and receiving the order, nearly half were dissatisfied with the enforcement process. Comments indicated that some law enforcement officers were reluctant to make arrests, seemed unfamiliar with the orders, or dismissed the women's fear and pleas for help. The orders did, however, appear to work well in the areas of protecting children, gaining a sense of control, reducing fear, and beginning the process of divorce.

The majority of women responding to the survey felt empowered by the protection order experience, describing positive changes in self-perception not necessarily tied to the practical effects of the orders. Acting on one's own behalf, moving away from helplessness, using the legal system, and sending a strong message to the abuser that abuse would not be tolerated were all mentioned as ways the process improved women's self-perception.

Improving the Protection Order Experience

Regardless of their empowerment abilities, orders without enforcement offer little protection and often increase women's danger by creating a false sense of security. Batterers routinely violate orders, especially if they believe there is no real risk of being arrested. For enforcement to work, courts need to monitor compliance, women must report violations, and law enforcement officials, prosecutors, and judges should respond sternly to reported violations.

Domestic violence requires a coordinated response from each part of the justice system, acting in collaboration with local social service and advocacy group representatives. Civil protection orders, as part of the solution, cannot be used and enforced fully by any one of these groups without cooperation from the others. For example, law enforcement officers may be reluctant to file reports or make arrests if they do not believe the prosecutors will follow through or that the judge will impose appropriate sanctions. . . .

The Violence Against Women Act of 1994 actually strengthens protection orders and, if actively enforced, may help lessen battered women's struggles. Under the act's "full faith and credit" provision, states are required to enforce each other's civil protection orders. The act also makes it a federal crime for a person to cross state lines with the intent to engage in conduct that violates a protection order, and it prohibits anyone subject to an order that meets certain specifications from possessing a firearm. Unfortunately, as of June 1996 there have been only fourteen prosecutions under the act's criminal provisions.

> "*Many women are unwittingly discovering that taking out a protection order against their husbands or lovers may actually incite violence—sometimes with tragic consequences.*"

Restraining Orders May Incite Domestic Violence

Gerald McOscar

Gerald McOscar is an attorney in Pennsylvania. In the following viewpoint, he maintains that restraining orders are frequently ineffective and unjust. He contends that a victim who seeks a restraining order may so anger an abusive partner that the batterer sometimes responds with deadly violence. In addition, McOscar argues, since restraining orders can be issued merely on the word of the alleged victim, they are frequently used by vengeful spouses to gain the advantage in divorce or custody cases. There are other legal recourses victims and their advocates can take to achieve justice in domestic violence cases, he asserts.

As you read, consider the following questions:
1. According to McOscar, why can restraining orders be effective yet inappropriate?
2. In the author's opinion, why does the law concerning protection orders work too well?
3. When is justice another form of abuse, according to McOscar?

Reprinted from "Slap Your Spouse, Lose Your House," by Gerald McOscar, *Women's Quarterly*, Spring 1997, by permission of *Women's Quarterly*, a publication of the Independent Women's Forum.

Critics of Philadelphia's Police Department applauded when a new, smaller, and lighter "official" flashlight was issued to its officers. The old, heavy, club-like flashlight had become a "weapon of opportunity" in the hands of officers and suspects alike.

Tragic Consequences

The same could be said about Pennsylvania's Protection from Abuse Act, a well-intentioned and useful weapon in the fight against domestic violence, but all too often a "weapon of opportunity" in the hands of vengeful spouses and opportunistic lawyers seeking to gain the upper hand in divorce and custody cases. Indeed indiscriminate use of the act, which allows a wife to obtain a "protection order" against her potentially violent mate, may be fueling the domestic violence it was designed to quell. As a result, many women are unwittingly discovering that taking out a protection order against their husbands or lovers may actually incite violence—sometimes with tragic consequences.

The murders of several Philadelphia-area women by their ex-husbands and lovers occurred within days or weeks of protection orders being issued. Stefan Stromberg and her mother were stabbed to death in April 1996 by Stefan's husband, Larry Stromberg, just two days after her protection order became final. That same month, Sheila Cody, a twenty-six-year-old Norristown resident, was stabbed to death in her home despite the protection order issued the previous February. In June 1996, Kirk Harris, 32, first turned a gun on his two-year-old son, Tivan, then himself, despite a protection order. In October and November 1996, at least three more Philadelphia women were murdered despite protection orders.

The Stromberg case is typical. Larry Stromberg's parents told reporters that he had never been in trouble until he met Stefan. In their eyes, he was a devoted husband and she an unfaithful wife. Neither side denies her extra-marital affair and abortion, nor that she penned her husband a love letter even after he had been served with the protection order. Stefan's attorney, meanwhile, blasted media coverage of the tragedy as "irresponsible at best and dangerous at worst."

She denounced Larry Stromberg's family for attempting to blame the dead wife for his abusive behavior, and worried that people would think that protection orders are useless pieces of paper. But she misses the point.

Protection orders are, in fact, effective in most cases (intimidation is an effective deterrent), but that doesn't mean they're appropriate in most cases. If Larry Stromberg was violent, as Stefan's lawyer alleges, he should have been in jail. If he was simply distraught over a crumbling marriage and an unfaithful wife, why was he being punished? We may never know whether the protection order pushed him over the edge, but if the end seems sadly preordained in some of these cases, it may be the indiscriminate use of protection orders that makes it so.

Cheap, Easy, and Unfair

So common are accounts of women being beaten (or worse) after obtaining protection orders that plans are afoot in Pennsylvania to make it an aggravating circumstance to intentionally violate an order and take a life in the process—essentially allowing for the imposition of the death penalty in first-degree murder cases. In the words of one suburban county district attorney, "this happens more frequently than you would think. The people who are supposed to be protected are being killed, and our purpose . . . is to prevent the killing."

The problem may not be that the law doesn't work, but that it works too well. Protection orders are intentionally convenient, cheap, and easy to obtain; but convenient, cheap, and easy justice comes at a price. The act contains civil remedies for criminal behavior ("bodily injury," "imminent serious bodily injury," "rape," "spousal assault"), but lacks the due process guarantees, the moral authority, and the persuasive force of the criminal law. A protection order is a legal hybrid, neither fish nor fowl.

Thus, a plaintiff who alleges immediate and present danger of abuse may, without a court hearing, be granted "such temporary order as [the court] deems necessary to protect the plaintiff or minor children," including "granting possession to the plaintiff of the residence . . . to the exclusion of the defendant by evicting the defendant. . . ." In layman's terms, a spouse or lover can find himself out on the street on nothing more than the word of an angry partner. By the time a hearing is held, reputations, careers, and families may be in ruin. Insult is added to injury when the charges are later dropped or dismissed (as is often the case).

Rarely is one person wholly to blame when a relationship turns sour, but in most cases it is the man who finds himself out on the street. The act expressly directs courts to offer assistance and advice to the accusers, but no such assistance is offered the accused. The army of counselors, advocates, and clerks who have become gatekeepers to the courthouse in abuse cases routinely counsel their clients on the finer points of the law. While such practices ensure job security and continued funding in the war against domestic violence, they do little to instill confidence in the justice system—indeed, a whole industry owes its existence to domestic violence.

© Kirk Anderson 1994. Reprinted with permission.

To eager advocates, "imminent serious bodily injury" can mean anything from a raised voice to a clenched fist. The lexicon of domestic violence now includes such vague terms as "verbal" and "psychological" abuse. One attorney routinely asks her clients, "How did this [the husband's behavior] make you *feel*?" Predictably, vagueness leads to subjectivity, rarely the best measure of another's guilt. Is "I'll kill you, bitch!" a curse, an expletive, a threat, or verbal abuse? Is a shoving match between father and son over the son's late hours an expression of loving concern, parental discipline, or abuse? No one knows for sure anymore.

Another Form of Abuse

Whatever its form, violence usually begets violence. Justice that doesn't contain some measure of restraint, fairness, common sense, and compassion isn't justice at all, just another form of abuse. Protection orders aren't the only weapon in the war against domestic violence. Lawyers, judges, and advocates have a wide range of options at their disposal, from criminal law at one end of the spectrum to counseling and mediation at the other. They need only set aside their predilections, prejudices, and political agendas and choose the legal weapon best suited for the circumstances.

Periodical Bibliography

The following articles have been selected to supplement the diverse views presented in this chapter. Addresses are provided for periodicals not indexed in the *Readers' Guide to Periodical Literature*, the *Alternative Press Index*, the *Social Sciences Index*, or the *Index to Legal Periodicals and Books*.

Gloria Allred	"It's Time for D.A.s to Get Tough on Domestic Violence," *Ms.*, July/August 1996.
Marcia Coyle	"Act II," *Ms.*, October/November 1999.
Raoul Felder and Anita K. Blair	"Domestic Violence: Should Victims Be Forced to Testify Against Their Will?" *ABA Journal*, May 1996.
Glamour	"License to Kill Women," April 1999.
Jennifer Gonnerman	"Welfare's Domestic Violence," *Nation*, March 10, 1997.
Linda Gordon	"Killing in Self-Defense," *Nation*, March 24, 1997.
Mark Hansen	"Crossing the State Line?" *ABA Journal*, May 1999.
George Lardner Jr.	"No Place to Hide," *Good Housekeeping*, October 1997.
Fredrica Lehrman	"Factoring Domestic Violence into Custody Cases," *Trial*, February 1996.
Annys Shin	"Gun Bills Catch Women and Kids in the Crossfire," *Ms.*, July/ August 1997.
Jeffrey R. Sipe	"Is Prosecution Best Defense Against Domestic Violence?" *Insight*, December 2, 1996. Available from 3600 New York Ave. NE, Washington, DC 20002.
Mark Thompson	"A Farewell to Arms," *Time*, October 6, 1997.
Craig D. Turk	"Violence Against the Constitution," *Weekly Standard*, March 29, 1999. Available from 1211 Ave. of the Americas, New York, NY 10036.
Cathy Young	"Domestic Violations," *Reason*, February 1998.

CHAPTER 4

How Can Society Help Victims of Domestic Violence?

Chapter Preface

Domestic violence advocates are frequently asked why a battered woman would stay in an abusive situation. Most women eventually do leave, but until they do, their reasons for staying depend upon each woman's individual circumstances. Some women stay because they believe they deserve the abuse, or because they have grown up with abuse and do not realize that healthy relationships do not include violence. But many others stay only because they have no place to go and no way to support themselves on their own. Self-sufficiency is difficult for women who have no skills, no money, little education, and children to take care of.

A federally funded program is attempting to give battered women in Kentucky the opportunities and strength they need to gain more control over their lives and leave their abusers. Supporters of Kentucky's Job Readiness Program (JRP) believe that women are at a social and political disadvantage in society and that women are at risk of domestic abuse unless the balance of power in a relationship is equal. Advocates of the JRP assert that teaching women how to become self-sufficient will allow them to decide whether and when they should leave abusive situations. When a couple knows that a woman can leave a relationship at any time, supporters contend, the woman gains some of the power and control in a relationship.

The program helps abused women living in one of Kentucky's sixteen battered women's shelters become independent by providing remedial education, job training, employment, housing, child care, living skills, and legal assistance, among other services. The JRP program also helps the women with transportation problems, food, clothing, personal needs, equipment necessary for work, money management, self-esteem classes, and advocacy.

Kentucky's Job Readiness Program—and the long-term goal of empowering women in society—is one way of encouraging battered women to break free from their violent relationships. The viewpoints in the following chapter explore other approaches to helping victims of family violence.

"The [batterers'] groups clearly demonstrate that failing to confront batterers makes them worse."

Therapy Programs for Batterers Are Effective at Reducing Domestic Violence

Craig Chalquist

Craig Chalquist is a marriage and family therapist who supervises therapy groups for men convicted of battering women in Ventura County, California. In the following viewpoint, Chalquist maintains that group therapy for batterers gives men the opportunity to confront and change their behavior and attitudes. The first step in the process of breaking the cycle of violence against women, Chalquist contends, is to make the batterers understand that they alone are responsible for their behavior. Next, he asserts, the batterers are taught how to control their anger. According to Chalquist, long-time participants in the therapy groups are very effective in helping newer members own up to their responsibility and move beyond violence.

As you read, consider the following questions:
1. According to the author, what are some of the excuses used by batterers to explain their violence?
2. In Chalquist's opinion, how is a batterer who permits his wife to abuse him actually abusing her?
3. Why must all former batterers still continue to consider themselves batterers?

"The place of the 'masters of return' cannot be attained even by the completely righteous." That is to say, no man stands higher than the one who took the wrong way and then returned; not even the angels stand higher, according to another Talmudic saying.

—Erich Fromm, *You Shall Be As Gods*

"What you're saying," I interrupted, "is bullshit."

Men new to the therapy program for court-referred batterers run by Scott Barrella, MFCC [marriage, family, and child counselor], are fond of excusing their violence: it was the victim's fault; society's; alcohol's; my medication's; my childhood's; my parents'; the school system's; the justice system's; "it's my nature's.". . .

"Which are factors," I told the group's newest member, "but you're leaving out what you do with them, which in your case is to go to violence. Nothing and no one is responsible for that choice but you, and if you don't get off your victim-thinking and face that, you'll get plenty of time to think it over elsewhere . . . and a new set of friends who will be delighted to meet you."

Most of the men in our groups have already done time, Ventura County [California] law enforcement well aware that battery victims seldom press charges. As a result, the violence we hear about spans the gamut from pushing and grabbing to murder. One man will report backhanding a partner, another committing rape, another frightening a victim into near-fatal cardiac arrest. All are required to read their police reports to the group, a practice that begins to clear away the initial denial and minimizing of the crime.

"It didn't happen this way—"

"Yes, yes; read on without the explanations."

Although we begin by having them sign a strict contract (they're usually referred by Probation for a mandatory fifty-two weeks), informing their victims, and teaching them how to identify critical moments (where they feel pumped enough to lose control), take time-outs, say "jail" to themselves, catch themselves being controlling, and other containment techniques, the real power of the approach developed by Scott ignites in the group process itself.

To illustrate:

In one of the first groups I attended, I was astonished to see an old soldier turn to a man just shy of his 20's and ask, "What are you doing here? Look at you: you're young, you're a good-looking guy, you're bright. . . . I'm an old fart, though a nonviolent one now thanks to what I've learned here. But you—you have your whole life ahead of you! Don't be an idiot and sit it out in jail."

A new man jeered about "teaching that bitch a lesson"; Scott stood and role-played the incident with him. "How did you hit her? Show me. Is this what you've done with your other victims? How did they react? What was your self-talk at the time?" He then polled the group for comments: "You sure have a way with women, bud." "You taught her a lesson all right—to call the cops when you're violent with her." "You laugh, but how do you feel about what you did?" "You belong here."

Anger and Denial

The groups clearly demonstrate that failing to confront batterers makes them worse. Scott asked one man, "When did you last speak to your wife?" (who had filed a restraining order against him). After the barest hesitation the man said, "During the arrest."

"So when I call her after the session, she'll tell me the same thing?"

The man glared in pretended outrage; Scott asked if anyone believed he didn't violate the restraining order. No one did, and in the next session the man confessed that in addition to the arrest details given previously, he also slapped his wife three times during the incident. The group praised him for opening up . . . and suggested he continue "remembering" in future sessions.

One would think that batterers have no problem being angry, but they do. To a man they stuff their anger so well that it can only emerge explosively. To a roofer humiliated by his boss but taking it "philosophically," Scott replied, "I'm not buying it. With your history you'd have to be angry. Where is it going? Tell us about the rest of your day." Well, nothing special . . . except a bit of mayhem at the construction site and a drinking bout after. Time for a review of watching for critical moments, staying sober, making assertive requests, and channeling rage.

Other typical situations in our groups:

A pontificator giving advice on another man's problem is told by the group he's in fixer mode and needs to shut up and listen.

A husband who pretends that his distancing from his angry wife is an act of consideration is told he's controlling her by threatening her with abandonment.

A bouncer who can't understand why people think he's dangerous is told he's six feet tall and has biceps like bowling balls and a glare like Clint Eastwood's—"And where are you coming from with that, anyway?"

A man asking about other men's arrest incidents is asked to describe the details of his own.

A man complaining about the police is reminded that he's the one in a batterers' group.

A new member swearing that he only grabbed his partner to "protect" her is told he's full of it and in denial: "No offense. I was like you when I first got here. You'll learn."

A new member complaining about being treated like a criminal is told that he *is* a criminal.

A bully trying to browbeat the group suddenly finds an overlooked and even tougher batterer pointed out to him with the amused comment, "He has something he wants to say to you."

A group listening silently to an intimidator brag about his fighting prowess is asked, "Has he got you all so cowed that you're afraid to comment on his nonsense?"

A group talking up their horror of a well-publicized murderer is asked, "Why all the noise? This guy could be your patron saint."

Confronted, challenged, educated, frustrated, retrained, encouraged, and empathized with, men negotiate Scott's carefully prepared course while we watch carefully for incidents. Some learn self-control so well that one could tell the difference, even before entering the building, between a men's group and a batterers' group: the trucks, jeeps, and campers parked outside are the same, but the batterers' vehicles have broken windows, key scratches down the sides, missing windshield wipers, and other gifts from victims who now feel safe enough to vent their rage at the men who mistreated them. When the men come in with cuts or bruises, we ask them about it, then contact the victims to make sure the men weren't violent with them in turn. Many are not.

A New Type of Abuse

To a man who reported being insulted, spit at, and beaten up continually week after week:

"How clever of you to have found a new way to abuse your wife. You apparently don't see that letting someone mistreat you is abusive, not just to you, but to them."

He stared. The group went silent. Then he pointed at me. "Say that again."

"Letting your wife beat you is abusive to her. It encourages her to be inappropriately violent, increases her contempt for you, glorifies victimization, knocks down her self-esteem, and causes her guilt even if she consciously feels you deserve what you're getting."

Around the room men were nodding. I went on, "You're also setting yourself up to explode on her again. I'm all for atonement, but if you're going to go about it in this misguided fashion, at least be honest with yourself about what you're doing." He nodded, really thinking about it.

Men who've used the program as an opportunity to get a handle on themselves not only move beyond violence; they also become adept at identifying other new batterers. Often, when an ordinary-seeming convict on his first session walks into the room, our men look him over for a moment, then smile at each other and us and greet him: "Welcome, you've come to the right place." They see through sham and pretense, and any new participant, or for that matter any therapist, who makes the mistake of lying to himself or to them is in for quite a time.

Owning Up to Their Responsibility

They, and we, have occasionally seen men feel shallow remorse or tell us what they think we want to hear. Some just don't get it, and jail is the usual consequence. I believe in the right of a man to waste an important opportunity and screw up his life, and when he's given options and takes that course anyway I have no problem being finished with him. Struggling with any client who isn't invested in owning the work makes him worse, not better.

We've also seen men who began the journey with violence, arrest, jail time, victim-blaming, financial devastation, and the loss of relationships, jobs, and homes take the initiative one day and own their responsibility for how they live, give up their denial, quit justifying their crimes, quit being violent, quit drinking or using, work through old emotional baggage, leave partners who encourage abuse or are themselves batterers, obtain new careers, attend parenting classes, reconcile themselves with their families, enter loving relationships, go to school, counsel other men . . . and end up in higher, stronger, nobler places than they ever reached before. The peace and poise with which they sit in group shows everyone what commitment, courage, and painful self-work can achieve, and we often invite them back as volunteers.

Many therapists assume that self-examination and insight lead to responsibility and change. If anything, our men demonstrate the reverse. They come to us with ruined lives and destroyed self-esteem and are told that although society and their victims hate them, if anything, more than they hate themselves, they have a chance to turn themselves around. No matter how dominated they are by the multitude of pathogenic dynamics we know they suffer from, they are invited to use whatever freedom and energy and determination are left to them to get serious about moving forward while gathering self-knowledge, strength, and skills on the way. Without that first decision, that key commitment, whatever they learned would take them nowhere.

Courage and Humility

It takes courage, and humility, to know you're a mess and walk forward anyway. Our men have the added burden of having hurt loved ones. Walking forward requires keeping that burden in mind—because the men who think they're past it all are the ones who reviolate. A man who'd long been nonviolent was describing his past crimes when he was asked whether he still considered himself a batterer. He said yes because when you've battered previously, the potential is always there, and only by not being in denial about it can your vigilance really work. And he admitted in a sad, quiet tone that struck everyone who heard it, "I miss hitting people."

No matter how low he's sunk, a man can stand up again if he's serious about taking responsibility for learning how. In the end, being a Master of Return of any kind—and there are as many as there are people—is about choice. The man who makes it by default succumbs to himself. The man who makes and remakes it as consciously and seriously as he can scales heights unknown even to angels.

> "*There is no evidence at all that men who complete the [batterers'] programs treat their women any better than men who don't.*"

Therapy Programs for Batterers Are Ineffective at Reducing Domestic Violence

Margaret A. Hagen

In the following viewpoint, Margaret A. Hagen argues that therapy programs for male batterers do not prevent men from continuing to abuse women. Many programs for batterers are based on feminist theories that try to change men's attitudes toward power, control, and dominance, she asserts. However, Hagen contends, a program is said to be successful based solely on the batterer's word that he has changed. Furthermore, she adds, studies of these therapy programs have found that a significant number of abusers continued to be violent against their partners. Hagen is a professor of psychology at Boston University.

As you read, consider the following questions:

1. According to Hagen, what percentage of men arrested on charges of domestic violence in 1997 were ordered into counseling?
2. How has feminism supported the theory that batterers are also victims, in the author's opinion?
3. What is the Violence Risk Appraisal Guide, according to Hagen?

Reprinted, by permission, from "Bad Attitude," by Margaret A. Hagen, *National Review*, July 20, 1998. Copyright ©1998 by National Review, Inc., www.nationalreview.com.

When Wilfredo Cordero, an outfielder for the Boston Red Sox, was arrested for assault and battery against his wife in the summer of 1997, he never suspected he would be the indirect beneficiary of feminist theory. Allegedly Cordero, intoxicated, had struck his wife with a telephone, tried to choke her, and threatened to kill her. He pleaded guilty, and in exchange for a 90-day suspended sentence his attorneys assured the judge that he would receive domestic-violence counseling.

The next day, Cordero and his wife flew home to Puerto Rico. Within a month the couple had separated and his wife took out a restraining order against him. Cordero—who has been arrested for or accused of abuse by three different women—was saying, "I am well into my counseling program, and I realize the value of my counseling. I look forward to it helping me return to a normal life. I also look forward to returning to my baseball job." Soon enough, Cordero was back patrolling the outfield grass—this time for the Chicago White Sox at $1 million a year.

Gender Therapy

Cordero's case is typical. Of the 136,000 men arrested on charges of domestic violence in 1997, 86 per cent were ordered into counseling—either as the sole consequence of the arrest, or as a condition of probation or some other sentence. In those counseling programs, the treatment the men are most likely to get is "gender therapy," focused on eradicating the male need for power, control, and dominance.

Lenore Walker, the psychiatrist who developed the concept of battered-woman syndrome, is the chief advocate for the idea that batterers, in turn, are trapped in their socially conditioned role as controlling men. "A feminist political gender analysis has reframed the problem of violence against women as one of misuse of power by men who have been socialized into believing they have the right to control the women in their lives even through violent means," she wrote in a 1989 article. "The underbelly of interpersonal violence is seen as the socialized androcentric need for power."

This feminist analysis is buttressed by a more general victimology: not only are batterers the victims of their socialization, they are the unhappy sons of dysfunctional families with absent or abusive parents. Although some states have recently swung too far the other way (with mandatory arrest and prosecution for batterers whether or not the wife wants to press charges), in many states acts of domestic violence have effectively been decriminalized. Since a batterer suffers from a mental disorder, he requires therapy, not punishment ("Mr. Cordero, tell us how you feel.").

The leader in gender therapy is the Emerge program in Massachusetts. Established in 1977, Emerge is the oldest of the programs in this country and one of the largest, typically with 350 men enrolled at a time; it is generally considered a model for treating batterers. Explains Chuck Turner, co-director of Emerge, "We believe that men come into the program focused on their own feelings, needs, and concerns and with a sense of being entitled to subservience on the part of their partners. So, what we try to do in our educational program is to strengthen their awareness of the many forms of abuse, moving beyond physical abuse to look at psychological abuse, economic abuse, and sexual abuse as well as helping them develop the ability to understand the effect of their behavior on the feelings of their partners."

Treatment in programs like Emerge takes place in groups, where the presence of supportive fellow members is meant to diminish batterers' sense of isolation. Many groups begin each meeting with a recitation of each man's past and most recent violent acts. Success is usually measured by changes in attitude. A man who completes the program (half simply drop out) is asked if he feels differently about sex roles, anger, and control. If the answer is "yes," his treatment is considered successful.

No Evidence of Behavior Change

But do these "attitude changes" do anything to reduce violence? As Zvi Eisikovits and Jeffrey Edleson point out in their 1989 review of the literature in the field, "Most of the studies have been conducted by the very people who have designed the intervention and thus should be regarded as self-evaluations at best." Some show that men who complete the programs are marginally less likely to be rearrested than men who don't. But there is no evidence at all that men who complete the programs treat their women any better than men who don't.

Useless and Dangerous

A couple of days ago . . . I sat with a girlfriend and excitedly explained some of the pioneering techniques used to re-educate violent men. . . .

The subject of my enthusiastic rantings was a book called *Breaking the Cycle*, the product of eight years of scientific study by John Gottman and Neil Jacobson into the pathology of batterers and their partners. Their research is the first to take a scientific (as opposed to psychoanalytic) approach to violent relationships. . . .

Alongside discussions of the accountability of batterers (absolute, whatever the circumstances), whether women batter men (none were found in the study, although many women hit back in self-defence), and why women don't leave (actually most do, but leaving increases the risk of a violent attack), Gottman and Jacobson present a deeply complex portrait of the men involved. They concluded that the fashion for offering batterers counselling and therapy is at best useless, at worst actively dangerous; not only do men quickly learn to "talk the talk" and say what people want to hear, but it becomes too easy to forget that batterers are criminals, not patients.

Hettie Judah, *(London) Independent on Sunday*, June 28, 1998.

One of the soundest studies (it was not a self-evaluation) compared batterers who had been treated to ones who had not been treated and found that after a six-month program about one-quarter of each group remained non-violent for six months. About one-quarter of each group shoved, bit, or slapped their partners within that time period. About 15 per cent of those treated burned their partners, punched them unconscious, or threatened them with a weapon, as opposed to 22 per cent of the untreated. These are not encouraging numbers.

A recent eight-year study by Neil Jacobson and John Gottman of the University of Washington produced similar results; the authors concluded that the counseling programs are a waste of time. In fact, not only is there no reliable evidence that batterers' programs affect subsequent battering; there is no evidence that the counselors can even tell the difference between failure and success.

Using Risk Assessment to Determine Treatment

There is a method of risk assessment that appears to do better at distinguishing between inveterate batterers and men who committed acts of violence which they are unlikely to repeat. A research team in Ontario has identified a set of objective actuarial variables—including age of earliest violent offense and separation of parents before the age of sixteen—that have a demonstrable correlation with future violence. A program based on their methods—called the Violence Risk Appraisal Guide—is used throughout the forensic system in Ontario to help determine who can benefit from counseling and who had better be put in jail. The same idea is also being used as part of the Special Commitment Center program in Washington state for sex offenders deemed unrehabilitated after serving prison time.

"We've not been very successful at the control part of wife assault, " says Dr. Marnie Rice, head of the research team. "But we could probably do a lot better job of prediction." Which certainly makes more sense than programs based on the misguided feminist theory of re-education.

In 1993, Police Officer Curtis Wilson of Brockton, Massachusetts, handcuffed his wife, put a loaded gun to her head, threatened to kill her, and knocked her unconscious. Wilson was suspended and forced to surrender his service weapon. Upon his completion of a batterers' program, two counselors pronounced him no longer dangerous. The police returned his service revolver. In September 1995, Wilson shot and killed his wife and himself. His "social attitudes" evidently needed some more adjusting.

"As the welfare 'reform' goes into effect . . . domestic violence victims will be among those hardest hit."

Welfare Reform Must Include an Exemption for Victims of Domestic Violence

Jennifer Gonnerman

Under the welfare reform law passed by Congress in 1996, welfare recipients may receive benefits for a limited time before being removed from the benefits rolls. In the following viewpoint, Jennifer Gonnerman argues that battered women, many of whom receive welfare benefits, may need more time to become self-sufficient and get off welfare. She asserts that abusers frequently make it difficult for the women they batter to complete their education or find and maintain employment. Therefore, she contends, it is critical that the states adopt a Family Violence Option, which permits abused women to be exempted from the stringent requirements of the new welfare reform law. Gonnerman is a staff writer at the *Village Voice*, a weekly alternative newspaper in New York City.

As you read, consider the following questions:

1. What percentage of women who received Aid to Families with Dependent Children said they had been abused by their partner, according to a study cited by the author?
2. How many states have adopted the Family Violence Option, according to Gonnerman?
3. In Gonnerman's opinion, what other provisions of the welfare reform law unfairly penalize battered women?

Reprinted, with permission, from "Welfare's Domestic Violence," by Jennifer Gonnerman, *The Nation*, March 10, 1997.

When Bernice Haynes tried to get off welfare by enrolling in a job training program, her boyfriend tossed her textbooks in the trash. He refused to watch their two children while she was in class. And he would pick fights with her when she tried to study.

"Before the final exam, we fought all weekend from Friday to Monday morning," says Haynes, 31, who lives on Chicago's West Side. Haynes never got the chance to open her books over the weekend. "When I went in that Monday, I was exhausted—from the constant verbal abuse, the put-downs, from trying to keep myself alive—that test wasn't on my mind." She flunked. Haynes, who had been attending classes for a year and was trying to become a licensed nurse, was kicked out of the program—just twelve weeks before graduation.

The Link Between Domestic Violence and Welfare

Haynes is one of thousands of domestic violence victims whose abusive partner tried to thwart her efforts to escape poverty. And for women in the same situation, this struggle is about to get much tougher. The most comprehensive study to date—conducted by the Washington State Institute for Public Policy—found that 60 percent of women on Aid to Families with Dependent Children (A.F.D.C.) said they had been physically abused by their boyfriend or spouse at some point. The Better Homes Fund, a Massachusetts nonprofit, recently studied 409 women on A.F.D.C. and found that 63 percent reported being assaulted by their male partner.

As the welfare "reform" goes into effect and A.F.D.C. is abolished, domestic violence victims will be among those hardest hit. The new welfare legislation includes strict time limits governing how quickly recipients must move from welfare to work. But "it's potentially dangerous for domestic violence victims," says Jody Raphael, director of the Chicago-based Taylor Institute, who was one of the first people to study the relationship between household abuse and welfare. "It's predicated on the idea that women become dependent and lazy and really just need a kick in the butt to get out into the labor market. But if you're a past or current domestic violence victim, it'll be exceedingly difficult.

Women need support and time to get out of the [abusive] relationship, which they're not going to have under the bill."

The welfare bill's strict time limits range from two months to five years and dictate how long recipients have to find a job, enroll in a training program or start community service before being erased from the welfare rolls. "The rigidity of time limits . . . is not going to be workable," says Martha Davis, legal director of the National Organization for Women (NOW) Legal Defense and Education Fund. It "is likely to result in human tragedy if women are stalked in the workplace but feel they can't change jobs or stop going to work . . . because they'll lose their benefits—or if women in abusive relationships feel they can't leave because there is no safety net for them any longer."

Across the country, activists are fighting to soften the blow of the welfare legislation by urging states to adopt the Family Violence Option as part of their plans. Sponsored by Senators Paul Wellstone of Minnesota and Patty Murray of Washington, this amendment to the 1996 welfare bill urges states to identify victims of battering, refer them to counseling and waive any requirements that unfairly penalize them. So far, twenty-four of the forty states that have submitted welfare plans adopted part or all of this provision or mentioned domestic violence. "The Family Violence Option is the first time in federal law that the connection between violence and poverty has been recognized," says Davis, who is lobbying hard for it. "Violence makes women poor and it keeps women poor. It's critical that states address that."

Sabotaged by Their Abusers

At first, Bernice Haynes didn't realize her boyfriend of thirteen years was sabotaging her efforts to get off welfare. She recalls justifying the "whuppings" she received by blaming herself. And she remembers how he used to dissuade her from studying. "I was going to give you some money" for dinner, he would say. "But you seem to think that book is more important. Well then, I just suggest you feed those kids with those books." After such a diatribe, Haynes would struggle to "make things right" by acquiescing in her boyfriend's demands and shutting her textbook. Eventually, she woke up to her own abuse and got rid of him. Now she is a case manager at a welfare-to-work program, helping other domestic violence victims make this transition.

From these women, Haynes hears now-familiar tales of boyfriends and husbands undercutting their efforts. "If she makes more money than him, then he doesn't feel like he has power over her. And he doesn't want to lose that power," says Carol Neal, 28, whose boyfriend used to hit her when she started working as a counselor in a Chicago welfare-to-work program.

© Joe Sharpnack 1998. Reprinted with permission.

Domestic violence lawyers, service providers and counselors across the country have collected similar anecdotes. "We see men sabotaging women's efforts both in job training and on the job—men who turn off alarm clocks so the woman oversleeps or who harass [her] through e-mail," says Lucy Friedman, executive director of Victim Services, a New York City nonprofit which used to run a job training program for domestic violence victims. Last year, the NOW Legal Defense and Education Fund interviewed twenty-five service providers in New York City and found that between 30 and 75 percent of women in their welfare-to-work programs are being abused at home.

Unfortunately, time limits are not the only aspect of the welfare bill that may be especially harmful to battered women. States may now impose a residency requirement, thus penalizing domestic violence victims who flee to another state to insure their safety. And cooperating with the new rule that requires welfare recipients to identify their children's father could put battered women in greater danger.

Proponents of the Family Violence Option are careful to point out that their goal is not to exempt these women permanently from the new work requirements. "We're just trying to provide them with more time and the specific services they need," Raphael says. Ultimately, a job may be exactly what some of these battered women need. "I believe work is often a stronger therapeutic tool than counseling," says Friedman. "It improves their self-esteem and can make them feel in control of their lives."

Identifying Domestic Violence Victims

While the Family Violence Option is supposed to protect domestic violence victims from the changes in welfare, precisely how it will accomplish this remains unclear. The first stumbling block is figuring out which welfare recipients are eligible for waivers. Maria Imperial, who oversaw a job training program for battered women at Victim Services, says, "I don't think many women are going to go into the welfare office and just say, 'I'm a domestic violence victim.'"

One of the first attempts to implement the Family Violence Option is a pilot program on Chicago's West Side, slated to start April 1, 1997. There, workers at the public aid office won't wait for women to announce that they're victims of domestic violence. Instead, the staff will tell female recipients that they may be excused from going to work within two years if it will put them in greater danger of abuse at home.

To find out about past and current abuse, the workers will ask four questions. The first inquires whether "someone in your life with whom you have or had a relationship" has engaged in "pushing, grabbing, shoving, slapping, hitting, restraining," among other abuses. If the woman answers yes, she is sent to a domestic violence counselor and may be exempted from some of the new welfare requirements.

Criticism of this program has yet to mount, although it is not difficult to imagine detractors insisting that some women will lie about being abused in order to stay on the welfare rolls. A more immediate hurdle, however, may be the general lack of awareness about domestic violence. While it is possible for states to waive welfare's time limits, it is not possible to legislate sensitivity.

Why Welfare-to-Work Programs Will Fail

Meanwhile, experts warn that if states do not attempt to tackle domestic violence from the outset by granting waivers to those who need them, their welfare-to-work programs will fail. Martha Baker, the executive director of Nontraditional Employment for Women, learned this lesson first-hand. Her Manhattan-based program trains women on welfare to work in plumbing, construction and other blue-collar jobs. Baker estimates that 50 percent of her clients are being abused at home—and she encourages them to confront this issue before joining the work force. Otherwise, she says, the problem "rears its ugly head. And once it does, the women are in danger of losing their jobs because they're not showing up, or they come in looking like they've had the stuffing beat out of them, or they have some guy coming around who looks like a stalker."

4

"*Current welfare law . . . already makes provisions for women who can legitimately show they need more time to get off welfare, including victims of domestic abuse.*"

Welfare Reform Should Not Include an Exemption for Victims of Domestic Violence

Sally L. Satel

Domestic violence advocates are urging states to adopt the Family Violence Option (FVO) which would exempt battered women from the time limit restrictions enacted under the welfare reform passed of 1996. In the following viewpoint, Sally L. Satel argues that the FVO is unnecessary since current welfare law already exempts people—such as victims of domestic violence—who need more time to get off welfare. Satel asserts that an amendment that exempts abused women from welfare's time limit restrictions may cause the women's partners to persist in beating them in an attempt to continue receiving the welfare benefits. Satel is a psychiatrist and lecturer at the Yale School of Medicine and a member of the National Advisory Board of the Independent Women's Forum, a conservative women's advocacy group.

As you read, consider the following questions:

1. As cited by the author, what percentage of welfare recipients are exempt from the welfare reform act's work requirements in 1998 and 2002?
2. In Satel's opinion, why is the definition of "domestic violence" too broad?

Reprinted from "The Abuse Excuse," by Sally L. Satel, *Women's Quarterly*, Winter 1998, by permission of the *Women's Quarterly*, a publication of the Independent Women's Forum.

F eminist organizations usually support any government action that would put more women in the workforce—except when those women are on welfare. In their current battle to gut welfare reform, women's groups may have found an effective weapon in battered women.

The National Organization for Women says that holding abused women to the requirements of welfare reform— those that insist recipients work and end their benefits after five years—will put them in even further jeopardy. How? Forcing these women to leave their apartments to go to a job, NOW says, increases the opportunity for violent ex-lovers to stalk them. The group also insists that battered women shouldn't be held to the same work schedules as other welfare recipients because their abusive mates might prevent them from getting out the door in the morning, or these women might be embarrassed to show up with a black eye. "For a woman who is already in danger, enforcing the [work requirement and cut-off] would be like making her stand on a trap door," says Kim Gandy, executive vice president of NOW.

NOW and other women's organizations support a new bill that would, if passed by legislators, permit thousands of women on welfare to opt out of the reforms. The Murray-Wellstone Amendment on Domestic Violence would permit states to exempt victims of domestic violence from both the five-year cash cut-off and the work requirement.

Exemptions for Domestic Abuse Victims

Current welfare law, however, already makes provisions for women who can legitimately show they need more time to get off welfare, including victims of domestic abuse. As it is, seventy percent of the entire caseload is already exempted from work requirements in 1998. In 2002, when the reforms are fully implemented, half the caseload will still be eligible for exemption. In addition, when the five-year-limit on cash assistance takes effect in 2001, states can still exempt twenty percent of their caseload for "as long as necessary," again including abuse victims.

If anything, the amendment puts abused women at even greater risk by turning these women into cash cows for their deadbeat lovers. Consider: a mother and her children are living with a shiftless lout who sponges off her government check, food stamps, and Section 8 apartment. He learns that battered women can keep getting their benefits. If keeping his partner brutalized means a regular check for him, some men will do just that.

What the amendment does, furthermore, is to encourage welfare recipients to turn every altercation between intimates into a documented police emergency. If states require evidence of an arrest, imagine how many households will be calling 911 over minor skirmishes or made-up incidents. What will happen to the real victims of domestic violence if police become cynical over women crying wolf?

Finally, the proposal's impossibly broad definition of "domestic violence"—including "mental abuse"—means that virtually every woman who wants to can qualify for a temporary waiver from her work requirements. Such requirements "neglect to consider the time . . . that emotional injuries need to heal," says Gandy. By that logic, a woman who has suffered anguish of any kind should get a pass—for instance, if she claims she's feeling a little too upset to work one day. Yes, there may be times when real victims need a break. But they already have that under current law.

A Heavy Blow

Despite this, the Senate passed Murray-Wellstone ninety-eight to one in September 1997. If Murray-Wellstone succeeds, it could inflict a heavy blow to welfare reform. For groups like NOW, who claim that workfare is "slavery," that would be a sweet victory. But for mothers on welfare it would be an extraordinary setback. Escaping the rolls means independence for women; a dual freedom from the parasitic men in their lives and the welfare trap. Isn't this what feminism should stand for?

Periodical Bibliography

The following articles have been selected to supplement the diverse views presented in this chapter. Addresses are provided for periodicals not indexed in the *Readers' Guide to Periodical Literature*, the *Alternative Press Index*, the *Social Sciences Index*, or the *Index to Legal Periodicals and Books*.

Pam Belluck — "Shelters for Women Disclosing Their Locations, in Spite of Risk," *New York Times*, August 19, 1997.

Rosemary Black — "Domestic Violence: Why It's Every Woman's Issue . . . and What You Can Do," *American Health for Women*, March 16, 1997.

Paul A. Cedar — "Abused Women: How Can the Church Help?" *Moody*, September 1995. Available from 820 N. LaSalle Blvd., Chicago, IL 60610.

Garry Cooper — "Breaking the Cycle of Violence," *Family Therapy Networker*, January/February 1999. Available from 8528 Bradford Rd., Silver Spring, MD 20901.

Felicia Collins Correia — "Domestic Violence Can Be Cured," *USA Today*, November 1997.

Catherine Elton — "Father Knows Best," *New Republic*, March 24, 1997.

Rona Fernandez and Lucia Hwang — "Safety in Numbers," *Third Force*, July/August 1997.

Jennifer Bingham Hull — "After Abuse: Surgeons Help Erase the Scars," *Ms.*, January/February 1998.

Tamara Jones — "The Woman Who Can't Stop Crying," *Good Housekeeping*, June 1997.

Thomas Fields Meyer — "Haven Sent," *People*, November 23, 1998.

Rinku Sen — "Between a Rock and a Hard Place," *Colorlines*, Spring 1999.

Barbara Wickens — "Seeing Pet Abuse as a Warning," *Maclean's*, October 26, 1998.

Mary Sikes Wylie — "It's a Community Affair," *Family Therapy Networker*, March/April 1996.

For Further Discussion

Chapter 1

1. Philip Jenkins contends that the seriousness of domestic violence has been exaggerated because the definition of "abuse" has been trivialized to include such acts as "intimidation," "using male privilege" and "raising one's voice in anger." In your opinion, should the definition of domestic violence include only physical conduct, or should verbal or psychological abuse be included as well? Explain your answer.

2. Philip W. Cook asserts that men who are abused by their female partners do not need shelters. Murray Straus, quoted by Christine Wicker, agrees. On what other points do Cook and Straus agree? On what points do they disagree?

3. Mike Royko argues that domestic violence is not a serious problem for gay males because it is much easier for a gay man to leave a relationship than it is for a woman to leave her husband. Based on your readings in this chapter, do you agree or disagree with his assertion? Support your answer.

Chapter 2

1. Jerry P. Flanzer and Larry W. Bennett argue about whether or not alcohol abuse causes domestic violence. On what points do they differ? On what points do they agree? Which argument is stronger? Explain your answer.

2. Viviane Lerner contends that society has encouraged men to oppress and abuse women for thousands of years. Give some examples of how society once sanctioned violence against women. Although society's views on violence against women have changed, Lerner contends that men continue to beat women because they are physically stronger than women and because there is little public condemnation of their actions. Mona Charen, on the other hand, argues that society and the police are too quick to judge men guilty of battering; she maintains that patriarchy cannot be responsible for domestic violence since women are the aggressors just as frequently as men are. In your opinion, are Charen's objections valid? Why or why not?

Chapter 3

1. Frank S. Zepezauer argues that the Violence Against Women Act discriminates against men because its programs are geared toward helping mainly women. Based on your readings of the

viewpoints in this book, do you agree or disagree with his assertion? Explain your answer.

2. Julian Leigh and Janell D. Schmidt and Lawrence W. Sherman debate the deterrent effects of arrest on domestic violence. On what points do they agree? On what points do they differ? Which argument is stronger? Support your answer.

Chapter 4

1. Margaret A. Hagen contends that many batterers who participate in therapy groups are said to be "cured" by the group's facilitator based merely on the abuser's word that he has changed. How does Craig Chalquist respond to this concern? Does Chalquist's argument supporting group therapy convince you that the treatment is dependable? Why or why not?

2. Jennifer Gonnerman argues that welfare reform will trap women in abusive situations and therefore an amendment should be passed to exempt battered women from the law's new requirements. Sally L. Satel contends, however, that a new amendment is unnecessary because battered women are already exempt from the welfare law's requirements. What evidence does each author give to support her viewpoint? Which argument seems stronger? Defend your answer.

3. The authors in this and the previous chapter discuss a variety of approaches for preventing domestic violence. Based on your readings in this book, which solutions do you believe are most effective? What other programs do you think might reduce domestic violence? Explain your answers.

Organizations to Contact

The editors have compiled the following list of organizations concerned with the issues debated in this book. The descriptions are derived from materials provided by the organizations. All have publications or information available for interested readers. The list was compiled on the date of publication of the present volume; the information provided here may change. Be aware that many organizations take several weeks or longer to respond to inquiries, so allow as much time as possible.

AABL/The Northwest Network of Bisexual,
Trans and Lesbian Survivors of Abuse
PO Box 22869, Seattle, WA 98122
(206) 568-7777 • fax: (206) 325-2601
e-mail: info@aabl.org • website: http://www.aabl.org
AABL (Advocates for Abused and Battered Lesbians)/The Northwest Network provides counseling, support, legal advocacy, and housing assistance to lesbian, trans- and bisexual victims of domestic and dating violence. It publishes the journal *Voices*.

Batterers Anonymous (BA)
8485 Tamarind, Ste. D, Fontana, CA 92335
(714) 355-1100
Batterers Anonymous is designed to rehabilitate men who abuse women. It aims to completely eliminate physical and emotional abuse and seeks positive alternatives to abusive behavior. It publishes a manual entitled *Self-Help Counseling for Men Who Batter Women*.

Emerge: Counseling and Education to Stop Male Violence
2380 Massachusetts Ave., Ste. 101, Cambridge, MA 02140
(617) 547-9879 • fax: (617) 547-0904
e-mail: emergedv@aol.com • website: http://www.emergedv.com
Emerge is a victim-advocacy organization that conducts research and disseminates information on the abuse of women from a male perspective. Publications available from Emerge include the article "Why Do Men Batter Their Wives?"

Independent Women's Forum (IWF)
PO Box 3058, Arlington, VA 22203-0058
(800) 224-6000 • (703) 558-4991 • fax: (703) 558-4994
e-mail: info@iwf.org • website: http://www.iwf.org
The forum is a conservative women's advocacy group that believes that the incidence of domestic violence is exaggerated and

that the Violence Against Women Act is ineffective and unjust. It publishes the *Women's Quarterly.*

Men's Health Network (MHN)
PO Box 75972, Washington, DC 20013
(202) 543-6461 • fax: (202) 543-2727
e-mail: info@menshealthnetwork.org
website: http://www.menshealthnetwork.org
Men's Health Network is concerned with the physical and emotional well-being of men. MHN has established a national clearinghouse of resources pertaining to men's health issues. Its titles include the report "Domestic Violence: A Two-Way Street."

Men's Rights, Inc. (MR)
PO Box 163180, Sacramento, CA 95816
(916) 484-7333
e-mail: webmaster@mens-rights.org
website: http://www.mens-rights.org
Men's Rights believes that women are as likely as men to initiate violence within relationships. MR publishes the newsletter *New Release*, along with position papers and articles.

Movement for the Establishment of Real Gender Equality (MERGE)
10011 116th St., Ste. 501, Edmonton, AB T5K 1V4, CANADA
(403) 488-4593
e-mail: Ferrel.Christensen@ualberta.ca
website: http://www.taiga.ca/~balance/mergprin.html
MERGE contends that publicity about family violence is biased toward women and ignores the male victims of spousal abuse. MERGE disseminates educational information on gender issues, including the pamphlet *Balancing the Approach to Spouse Abuse* and its quarterly magazine *Balance.*

National Center on Elder Abuse (NCEA)
National Association of State Units on Aging (NASUA)
1225 I St. NW, Ste. 725, Washington, DC 20005
(202) 898-2586 • fax: (202) 898-2583
e-mail: ncea@nasua.org • website: http://www.gwjapan.com/NCEA
The National Center on Elder Abuse provides information, research, and technical training about elder abuse and neglect. Its Clearinghouse on Abuse and Neglect of the Elderly offers reports, articles, and other publications on elder abuse.

National Clearinghouse for the Defense of Battered Women
125 South 9th St., Ste. 302, Philadelphia, PA 19107
(215) 351-0010 • fax: (215) 351-0779
Created in 1987, the clearinghouse provides assistance, resources, and support to battered women who have killed or assaulted their abusers. Its publications include a newsletter entitled *Double-Time*.

National Coalition Against Domestic Violence (NCADV)
PO Box 18749, Denver, CO 80218-0749
(303) 839-1852 • fax: (303) 831-9251
website: http://www.ncadv.org
NCADV serves as a national information and referral network on domestic violence issues. Its publications include *Every Home a Safe Home*, *Teen Dating Violence Resource Manual*, the quarterly newsletter *NCADV Update*, as well as fact sheets on domestic violence, children and violence, and lesbian battering.

U.S. Department of Justice/Violence Against Women Office
810 7th St. NW, Washington, DC 20531
(202) 616-8894 • fax: (202) 307-3911 • hotline: (800) 799-7233
e-mail: bcampbel@justice.usdoj.gov
website: http://www.usdoj.gov/vawo/
The Violence Against Women Office leads a comprehensive national effort to combine tough new federal laws with assistance to states and localities to fight domestic violence and other crimes against women. Its publications include the *Domestic Violence Awareness Manual*, *A Community Checklist: Important Steps to End Violence Against Women*, and the monthly *Violence Against Women Act NEWS* newsletter.

Women's Freedom Network (WFN)
4410 Massachusetts Ave. NW, PMB #179, Washington, DC 20016
(202) 885-6245 • fax: (202) 885-1057
e-mail: wfn@american.edu
website: http://www.womensfreedom.org
WFN provides perspectives on family violence, sexual harassment, and other gender-related issues in its quarterly *Women's Freedom Network Newsletter*.

Bibliography of Books

Vera Anderson — *A Woman Like You: The Face of Domestic Violence.* Seattle, WA: Seal Press, 1997.

Frank Ascione and Phil Arkow, eds. — *Child Abuse, Domestic Violence, and Animal Abuse: Linking the Circles of Compassion for Prevention and Intervention.* Lafayette, IN: Purdue University Press, 1999.

Jeff Benedict — *Public Heroes, Private Felons: Athletes and Crimes Against Women.* Boston: Northeastern University Press, 1997.

Raquel Kennedy Bergen, ed. — *Issues in Intimate Violence.* Thousand Oaks, CA: Sage, 1998.

Ruth A. Brandwein, ed. — *Battered Women, Children, and Welfare Reform: The Ties that Bind.* Thousand Oaks, CA: Sage, 1999.

Eve S. Buzawa and Carl G. Buzawa, eds. — *Do Arrests and Restraining Orders Really Work?* Thousand Oaks, CA: Sage, 1996.

Philip W. Cook — *Abused Men: The Hidden Side of Domestic Violence.* Westport, CT: Praeger, 1997.

Richard L. Davis — *Domestic Violence: Facts and Fallacies.* Westport, CT: Praeger, 1998.

R. Emerson Dobash and Russell P. Dobash, eds. — *Rethinking Violence Against Women.* Thousand Oaks, CA: Sage, 1998.

Donald Alexander Downs — *More than Victims: Battered Women, the Syndrome Society, and the Law.* Chicago: University of Chicago Press, 1996.

Andrea Dworkin — *Life and Death: Unapologetic Writings on the Continuing War Against Women.* New York: Free Press, 1997.

Raoul Felder and Barbara Victor — *Getting Away with Murder: Weapons for the War Against Domestic Violence.* New York: Simon & Schuster, 1996.

Richard J. Gelles and Donileen R. Loseke, eds. — *Current Controversies on Family Violence.* Thousand Oaks, CA: Sage, 1993.

L. Kevin Hamberger and Claire Renzetti, eds. — *Domestic Partner Abuse.* New York: Springer, 1996.

Neil S. Jacobson and John M. Gottman — *When Men Batter Women: New Insights into Ending Abusive Relationships.* New York: Simon & Schuster, 1998.

Raymond M. Jamiolkowski	*Drugs and Domestic Violence.* New York: Rosen, 1996.
Jana L. Jasinski and Linda M. Williams, eds.	*Partner Violence: A Comprehensive Review of 20 Years of Research.* Thousand Oaks, CA: Sage, 1998.
Catherine T. Kennedy and Karen R. Brown	*Report from the Front Lines: The Impact of Domestic Violence on Poor Women.* New York: NOW Legal Defense and Education Fund, 1996.
Ethel Klein et al.	*Ending Domestic Violence: Changing Public Perceptions, Halting the Epidemic.* Thousand Oaks, CA: Sage, 1997.
Alison B. Landes, Suzanne Squyres, and Jacquelyn Quiram, eds.	*Violent Relationships: Battering and Abuse Among Adults.* Wylie, TX: Information Plus, 1997.
S. Rutherford McDill and Linda McDill	*Dangerous Marriage: Breaking the Cycle of Domestic Violence.* Old Tappan, NJ: Spire Books, 1998.
Alice Myers and Sarah Wight, eds.	*No Angels: Women Who Commit Violence.* New York: HarperCollins, 1997.
Patricia Pearson	*When She Was Bad: Violent Women and the Myth of Innocence.* New York: Viking, 1997.
Claire M. Renzetti and Charles Harvey Miley, eds.	*Violence in Gay and Lesbian Domestic Partnerships.* New York: Haworth Press, 1996.
Albert R. Roberts, ed.	*Helping Battered Women: New Perspectives and Remedies.* New York: Oxford University Press, 1996.
Diana E.H. Russell	*Dangerous Relationships: Pornography, Misogyny, and Rape.* Thousand Oaks, CA: Sage, 1998.
Robert L. Snow	*Family Abuse: Tough Solutions to Stop the Violence.* New York: Plenum Press, 1997.
Mary Roth Walsh, ed.	*Women, Men, and Gender: Ongoing Debates.* New Haven, CT: Yale University Press, 1997.
Karen J. Wilson	*When Violence Begins at Home: A Comprehensive Guide to Understanding and Ending Domestic Abuse.* Alameda, CA: Hunter House, 1997.

Index